Index on Censorship

Free Word Centre, 60 Farringdon Road, London, ECIR 3GA

Volume 41 No 2 2012

If you are interested in republishing any article featured in this issue, please contact us at permissions@indexoncensorship.org

Supported using public funding by
LOTTERY FUNDED | **ARTS COUNCIL ENGLAND**

PLAYING THE FIELD

Jo Glanville

Should sport be above politics and human rights? Formula One chief Bernie Ecclestone seems to think so. As calls for a boycott of the Grand Prix in Bahrain reached their height in April, he told reporters: 'It's nothing to do with us.' The attitude of international sports bodies towards engaging with authoritarian regimes can range from brazen disregard for the country's human rights record to idealistic notions of sport as a force for good. As Mihir Bose recalls in this issue of *Index*, the International Olympic Committee (IOC) skirted the question when it came to awarding the bid to Beijing in 2001 and then rashly promised that China would emerge a more open society [pp. 48-55].

The modern history of sport as a universally improving pursuit goes back to the 19th century novel *Tom Brown's Schooldays*, Bose goes on to reveal, but it's the potential for propaganda and investment that has always been the draw for dictatorial world leaders. President Putin is getting ready to host the 2014 Winter Olympics in Sochi, on the edge of the deeply troubled North Caucasus. Arnold van Bruggen and Rob Hornstra are in the midst of an inspired five-year project documenting Moscow's unstable backyard: a catalogue of devastation that sits uncomfortably alongside Putin's ambitions for showcasing Russia [pp. 94-101]. Further west, Belarus's dictator Alexander Lukashenko is looking forward to indulging his passion for ice hockey when the country hosts the world championship in the same year. There are currently calls to boycott the Belarus event. If the championship does go ahead in Minsk, for civil society 'it will be yet another insult' writes Natalka Babina [pp. 102-109].

During the apartheid era, the International Olympic Committee took a hard line against South Africa, banning the country from taking part in the Games. While there seems less appetite today for taking a political stand, even in such a morally clear-cut case, there were strong differences

Relay finals at the 1948 Olympic Games, Wembley Stadium, London, 7 August 1948
Credit: Press Association

SAQI BOOKS
Understanding the Middle East in Revolt

VYING FOR INFLUENCE IN THE NEW EGYPT

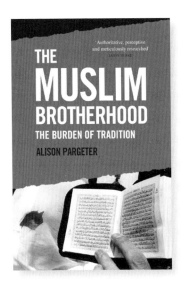

The Muslim Brotherhood: The Burden of Tradition
Alison Pargeter

'Alison Pargeter has established a reputation as one of the best current analysts of Islamic radicalism. This book – detailed, authoritative, sober, perceptive and meticulously researched – shows why. It is an important contribution to our understanding both of the Muslim Brotherhood itself, to the controversies that surround the movement and to the broader phenomenon of political Islam. A must read for scholars, students and anyone interested in the Middle East.'
Jason Burke

£20 | 978-0-86356-475-8

EXAMINING THE DEMOCRACY DEFICIT IN THE ARAB WORLD

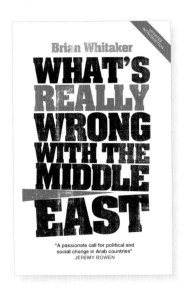

What's really wrong with the Middle East
Brian Whitaker

'A passionate call for political and social change in Arab countries' Jeremy Bowen

'[Should] be required reading by Arab elites from the Atlantic to the Gulf' *Al Hayat*

'A passionate attack on the corrosive effects of inequality' *New Statesman*

£10.99 | 978-0-86356-624-0

www.saqibooks.com

of opinion at the time. Celebrated South African playwright Athol Fugard spoke out against both cultural and sporting boycotts in 1973, in an interview republished in this issue: 'My view is that a boycott psychology is a bomb psychology. One solution to the South African problem is to drop a bloody great hydrogen bomb on the country, blow the whole thing to ashes . . . I'm not interested in that. I'm interested in the survival of what I know is still there, vital and intact' [pp. 56-58].

In London's Olympic year, it's the growing power of the brand that has been causing particular concern. The rules and regulations accompanying the Games are ripe for comedian Natalie Haynes's parody: commenting on the sweeping legislation that prohibits unauthorised bodies from using images, words and even sounds associated with the Olympics, she writes: 'What, you may be wondering, is the sound of the Olympics? The gentle flow of tenners as they sink into an open drain?' [pp. 66-69]. In a fascinating account of early offshoots of the Games, Martin Polley and Stephen Escritt demonstrate how the desire for Olympic control is directly linked to the rise of commercial sponsorship [pp. 59-65]. You can read the civil rights group Liberty's concerns about some of the very broadly framed legislation that has been passed to protect the Olympic brand, along with recent bye-laws limiting the right to protest [pp. 88-91].

Also in this issue, you can read former Czech dissident and novelist Ivan Klíma's engaging satire of communist sporting prowess, first published in *Index* in 1981 when he was still a banned writer; an interview with acclaimed Syrian cartoonist and *Index* award-winner Ali Ferzat, and poetry from Sri Lanka along with reports on news and culture from Hungary, Dagestan and India.

For the rest of the year, thanks to our publisher SAGE, you can read *Index*'s archive from 1972–2010 for free at www.indexoncensorship. org/magazine-archive to mark our 40th birthday and take advantage of a 40 per cent discount on your 2012 subscription to the magazine at www.indexoncensorship.org/subscribe. Read daily reports on censorship and free speech on our website (www.indexoncensorship.org) and visit the exhibition *Politics and Olympics* this summer at the Free Word Centre, 60 Farringdon Road, London EC1R 3GA, co-curated by Stephen Escritt. ❑

©Jo Glanville
41(2): 1/5
DOI: 10.1177/0306422012448766
www.indexoncensorship.org

CONTENTS

INDEX INDEX

A round-up of censorship in the UK

CULTURE CRUSH

Olympic rings, River Thames, London, 28 February 2012
Credit: Stephen Simpson/Rex Features

DISPATCHES

News from the front line:
Syria, Hungary, Dagestan and Greece

Credit: Ali Ferzat

CREATIVE DISSENT

Celebrated cartoonist **Ali Ferzat** has defied the Syrian regime's brutal methods to silence his satires. He talks to **Malu Halasa**

Three months before the start of the Syrian revolution in March last year, Ali Ferzat broke with his own satirical convention: he stopped using symbolism in his cartoons to criticise the regime and began to target identifiable individuals, including the president himself. He describes the shift as pushing through 'the barrier of fear'. The first cartoon in Ferzat's new series showed President Bashar al Assad agitated at seeing the traditional day of mass demonstrations against the regime, Friday, marked on a wall calendar. Another had him hitching a lift from Gaddafi making his own getaway in a car. The third featured the 'chair of power', one of Ali Ferzat's iconic symbols, with the springs popping out of the cushion and Bashar hanging onto its arm.

Drawing the president, Ferzat admits, was a personal and political breakthrough – if not foolhardy. 'It is quite suicidal to draw someone who is considered a godlike figure for the regime and the Ba'ath party, but still I did it and people respected that courage and started carrying banners with caricatures in the protest to show how they feel about things.'

Ferzat must have anticipated that his actions might lead to violent repercussions. Last August, pro-regime forces viciously assaulted him and

broke both his hands. During the attack, one of the assailants yelled at him, 'Bashar's shoe is better than you.' Article 376 of the Syrian penal code makes it an offence to insult or defame the president, and carries a six-month to three-year prison sentence.

The most lauded cartoonist of the Arab spring, Ferzat has won countless international prizes – including this year's Index Freedom of Expression Award for the Arts. For more than 40 years, he has been delivering his own scathing messages to dictatorship. Published daily in *al Thawra* (the Revolution) newspaper in Damascus for a decade, he was a thorn in the side of Hafez al Assad. In the early noughties, the launch of his satirical newspaper *al Doumari* (the Lamplighter) was considered a hopeful sign in the nascent presidency of Hafez's heir. Last December, when Bashar al Assad was asked about the attack on Ali Ferzat by the American news commentator Barbara Walters, he responded, 'Many people criticise me. Did they kill all of them? Who killed who?' Such comments made little sense and attest to Ferzat's power, whether convalescing in a hospital bed or through his drawings.

There are two cartoons by Ferzat embedded in my own visual consciousness of Syria during years of visiting and writing about the country. The first is a drawing of a man whose head has been sliced and popped open at the airport. Instead of searching the luggage on the rack, a uniformed authority figure inspects the contents of the man's brain. The other is of a dismembered prisoner hanging in a cell, body parts everywhere, while the jailer sits on the floor, sharp implements to hand, crying over a television soap opera. Both of them were a comment on the secret life that routinely takes place in Syria, the self-censorship that is sometimes needed to survive and the ongoing activities inside prisons that are rarely officially acknowledged in the state media.

In a recent exhibition of Ali Ferzat's work at the MICA gallery in London, there were numerous examples of his coded messages: the armchair of *salat* (representing ruling power), the shortened ladder to suggest the gulf between the political elite and the nobodies (sometimes in a hole) or the ever busy authority figure waving a roll of toilet paper like a flag. The messages are inescapably clear but their target is not always what one might expect. In one colourful drawing, a man is trying to pluck fruit from a tree, but the three ladders on which he is standing have been laid horizontally, not vertically. Pausing beneath this picture, Ferzat points out, 'Yes, I always speak truth to power. Sometimes it's not only the president to be blamed but the people too.' The gallery, usually closed at the weekend, was filled with Syrians and their families within minutes of its unscheduled opening. Everyone, from

Ali Ferzat accepts the Arts Award at the 2012 Index on Censorship Freedom of Expression Awards
Credit: Mark Green

grown men to children of all ages, photographed the cartoons on the walls with their mobile phones.

Ferzat's unique visual vocabulary, developed in extreme circumstances, has had an unexpected reach: 'To survive and get around censorship, my caricatures had to be speechless and rely instead on symbols. That gave them an international aspect I did not intend in the first place. So I managed to get the voice of people inside Syria to the outside, through channels of common human interest.'

During his stay in London in the spring, Ferzat received good news. There is an interest in reviving *al Doumari*, with plans to publish it in exile in Dubai and, ultimately, hopefully back home as well. One gets the impression that no matter where Ferzat is – he currently resides in Kuwait because his family thinks it is too dangerous for him to be in Damascus – living away from the revolution has been frustrating. He spends most nights watching the Arabic news channels and drawing until the early hours. His right hand,

which was fractured in the attack last summer, remains a little stiff, although that is not evident in the first two cartoons he drew when he was able to move his fingers. One shows an armoured Trojan warhorse with marauding tanks for hooves. The second is, again, a tank poised on its back wheels, ready to crush a lone green shoot sprouting from the ground.

The Syrian people are a major influence on his work. 'Drawing is first of all a means and not a purpose in itself,' he says. 'The artist is always the one who produces an idea, but if that person is not living within his community then how can he reflect what his community is going through? Art is about being with your own people and having a vision of what they need. You can't sit in your room isolated behind your window and draw about life – it doesn't work like that.' The revolution was sparked in March 2011 when young graffiti artists in Deraa, between the ages of nine and 15, were arrested and tortured for writing government slogans on the walls. The sale of spray paint is now banned in Syria unless ID papers are shown.

There have been many false springs in the country's turbulent political history. A decade ago, and just a few months after Bashar al Assad assumed the presidency, Syrian artists and intellectuals were hopeful that change was possible in their country, a sentiment that began in Ferzat's case when Bashar al Assad, a 'tall dude with a large entourage', walked into his exhibition filled with censored cartoons. (Ferzat always shows banned cartoons in his exhibitions.) When the new president asked Ferzat how he might be able to gauge popular opinion, the cartoonist urged him to simply talk to the people. Eventually Bashar telephoned him and said he was having a Pepsi with ordinary folk in the street. This was during the so-called Damascus spring of the early noughties, when the regime was courting artists and intellectuals. Imbued by optimism in 2001, Ferzat started his satirical newspaper *al Doumari*, but as the mood of the political elite reverted to tried and trusted methods, so did the fortunes of his weekly. By the time it closed in 2003, 105 issues later, he had survived two assassination attempts that were never investigated. Thirty-two court cases had been filed against the newspaper and advertisers had stopped advertising.

Historically, cartoonists have been astute in their circumvention of censorship. As Fatma Müge Göçek has shown, under the Ottoman press laws of the early 1900s, they sent erasable drawings to the censors and, after approval, substituted other images in their place. Newspapers at that time also appeared with black boxes where a cartoon had been censored. As the gap widened between official pronouncements and reality – or as Václav Havel once said, 'People know they are living a lie' – caricatures became an important means of expression in the Middle East. Now cyberspace provides a comparatively safe haven for pictures and ideas that cannot be expressed in print.

Editorial cartooning, like journalism, is considered a western invention, but the convention of satire in the Middle East is as old as the stories of *Alf Laila wa Laila* (A Thousand and One Nights). Ferzat's peers include the Egyptian Baghat Othman, who parodied Sadat, Palestinian Naji al Ali, creator of the Palestinian barefoot boy Hanzala (with his back always to the reader in rejection of the world around him) and Algerian Chawki Amari, now in exile in Paris after serving a three-year sentence in his country for drawing the country's flags in a cartoon that was seen as 'defacing' a national symbol. The Syrians also bring something new to the mix, which springs from a sense of humour coloured by the experience of dictatorship, coupled with sexual innuendo. This blend is nicely demonstrated by a joke from the 1980s that is still pertinent, as recently

told to me by a political activist. 'A guy used to talk about the president. The *mukhabarat*, secret police, picked him up and started beating and torturing him. They told him, "Stop making jokes about the president. Stop talking about the president. You can tackle whatever issues you want, but in the end you always have to say: this has nothing to do with the president. The president is not aware of this." So the minute the guy is released, he sees his family waiting by the door and says, "Have you heard, the wife of the president is pregnant and the president has nothing to do with it. He's not even aware of it."'

Even in his comic strips for juveniles, Ferzat has challenged traditional sensibilities in Syria, a country known for channelling propaganda through state-sponsored children's publications. Ferzat was 26 years old when he created 'The Travels of Ibn Battuta' for the popular *Usama* magazine, published in 1977. In the strip, the famous medieval Arab traveller Ibn Battuta is depicted with a moustache and beard, wearing a turban in the shape of the globe. Ferzat demystifies Ibn Battuta by drawing Muhammad Ali, Omar Sharif and the pop singer Abdel Halim Hafiz, with a turban globe on their heads; as avatars of Ibn Battuta, they respectively box, hug a leading lady and sing. Later in the strip, as the historic traveller pulls his donkey into the present day, his size shrinks, suggesting he is overwhelmed by modern life.

A letter sent to the editor of *Usama* complained about this portrayal of Ibn Battuta. Ferzat did not use one of the traditional Arab figures of ridicule such as the poet Abu Nuwas or the folk character Juha as his fumbling protagonist, but instead a notable historical personage, which the letter writer found highly insulting. This was at a time when the magazine was already starting to change, and was publishing less controversial material, as Allen Douglas and Fedwa Malti-Douglas show in their study of Arabic comic strips.

Originally from a Sunni Muslim family in Homs, Ferzat describes freedom of the press as 'a responsibility'. He stresses: 'It's not as if I should do whatever I feel like doing, regardless of the consequences. It is a matter of moral commitment at the end of the day and varies between countries, depending on the culture and civil liberties. You have to find the right balance. Some newspapers have no obligation, not even morally, and they refrain from nothing and then call it "freedom". Meanwhile other newspapers censor human interest stories. I see both as bad – whether too much suppression in the name of commitment, or too much unethical commitment in the name of freedom. They are both the same.'

During prolonged periods of dictatorship, there have been unexpected chinks in the wall of silence, which Lisa Weeden outlines in her tour de force *Ambiguities of Domination*. One way ordinary Syrians thwarted the cult of Hafez al Assad that pervaded their daily lives was in their choice of newspapers. Throughout the 1970s, *al Thawra* published a daily editorial cartoon by Ferzat. When he was dropped from the newspaper, *al Thawra* experienced a 35 per cent drop in sales and was forced to ask the cartoonist to return. Ferzat's stories about his days there are particularly amusing and they reveal just how much leeway can exist in what at first glance appears to be a monolithic system. In some instances, the offending cartoon would be published in the paper. Then the abusive phone calls from the minister of information would begin.

Ferzat continues, 'They came with this new procedure. First the editor-in-chief had to look at the caricature. If he approved it, he had to send it to the general manager. If he approved it, or if he found it controversial and difficult to understand, he had to send it to the minister of information. Take into consideration that the minister of information was a bit of an ass, he would say "Yes" because he didn't understand it and the next day the people would get the meaning because it only took commonsense. Suddenly the angry phone calls would start all over again.'

According to Italian visual critic Donatella Della Ratta, Bashar al Assad's Syria is ruled by what she calls 'a whispering campaign' waged by competing elites, the secret police, the official media and finally the president and his inner circle. All of the different factions are involved in censorship: it takes many pillars of society to control the flow of information and ideas in a totalitarian state.

In such a society, what is the difference between self-censorship and survival for someone like Ferzat? 'What I can tell you is that I have no boundaries,' he says. 'I don't have a censor or a policeman in my head before I draw. However, it is not requested of *fedayeen* – freedom fighters – to be suicidal. As an artist, I'm not going to go and find a landmine and sit on top of it. I invented the symbols that actually manipulate the censor and survive the dangers of punishment. I put simple codes and symbols in my drawings, and anyone who has the capacity to notice things would understand them. That is what I do to secure myself and not be suicidal.'

He concludes, 'At the end of the day, my drawings and caricatures are part of the daily culture of the street. I want to represent the consciousness of the street, of the people, and I do, and that gives my work value.'

As Ferzat and the graffiti artists of Deraa, who sparked a revolution over a year ago, have shown: Sharpie pens and spray paint can be the most effective tools against a brutal regime. ❐

©Malu Halasa
41(2): 14/25
DOI: 10.1177/0306422012447747
www.indexoncensorship.org

Malu Halasa is a writer and editor. Her books include *The Secret Life of Syrian Lingerie* (Chronicle Books)

HUNGARY'S BETRAYAL

A new media law is undermining press freedom and a long established liberal tradition. **James Kirchick** reports on the fallout

On 21 December 2010, at 6.15 in the morning, Attila Mong did something unusual for a radio host: he held a minute of silence. Mong, who had been working for less than a year at Mr1-Kossuth, one of Hungary's public, nominally independent radio stations, was protesting a law that would create a media authority with exceptionally wide-reaching powers. The media law, which took effect on 1 January, last year, less than two weeks after Mong's protest, is one of the most controversial measures to have been enacted by the conservative nationalist government of Prime Minister Viktor Orban. The Fidesz party came to power two years ago with an unprecedented two-thirds parliamentary majority and has clashed repeatedly with the European Union over claims that it is consolidating power and destroying checks and balances.

Immediately after the minute of silence, the studio began filling with the station's managers. When Mong's shift on the morning news programme ended, he was summoned before Mr1's bosses. He was suspended along with his producer, and an internal investigation was launched to discover whether the two had violated internal rules by airing their personal opinions. Ultimately, the investigation dragged on for months, until the expiry of Mong's contract.

Mong does not regret the risk he took. He has been a journalist for 15 years in Hungary, mostly for a private radio station in Budapest called Info Radio, and has written several books about white collar crime. 'I had this journalistic conscience problem, that I knew we had a media law which is a serious threat, the text is a serious threat,' he told me earlier this year over lunch at a Budapest restaurant. 'We don't want to have young reporters in 15 years time to come to us and ask, "What did you do when you were there? You were a leading journalist, you were on air, on the public radio, the most popular program on public radio." And I didn't want young people to ask this question.'

The law in question creates a regulatory body – all of whose members have been appointed by Orban's ruling Fidesz Party – that has the ability to impose crippling fines of up to $100,000 on journalists and news outlets for committing the nebulous misdeed of 'offending human dignity'. In response to criticism from the European Commission and European Parliament, and in an attempt to convince critics that the 56 new regulations were no more onerous than those imposed by the rest of Europe, the Hungarian government produced a detailed response comparing its media law to others across the continent. But a recent report by the Center for Media and Communication Studies at Central European University, relying upon experts in 20 European countries, found that 'in a majority of examples, experts report that the Hungarian government's references omit or inaccurately characterise relevant factors of the other countries' regulatory systems, and as a result, the examples do not provide sufficient and/or equivalent comparisons to Hungary's media regulation system'. In protest at the law, liberal Hungarian newspapers and magazines ran blank pages on their covers and on the homepages of their websites.

In addition to this, public service media has been purged of anyone suspected of harbouring critical views of the government and stacked with Fidesz loyalists. Such politicisation of state-funded media detracts from its professionalism; the BBC, so widely respected around the world, does not experience massive staff turnovers when a new government is elected. 'They are all from the right wing,' Mong tells me. 'Before the elections they were working for right-wing publications, right-wing radio, so [they are] very much loyalists. Mong is no partisan, however. 'You can find these kinds of people of course on both sides, on the left as well.' Yet the degree to which public media has become a mouthpiece for the government is unparalleled in Hungary's post-communist history.

During the previous, socialist-led government, the media was not nearly as politicised. As an example, Mong cites the fact that a 2006 speech delivered by the then prime minister to members of his party, in which he admitted that

Demonstration against the new media law, parliamentary building, Budapest, 14 January 2011
Credit: Laszlo Balogh/Reuters

the government had lied 'in the morning, at noon and at night', was a story first aired by public radio. 'Today it would be unimaginable to have a secret speech from Viktor Orban, and have the story broken by [public radio],' he says. The government is also able to exercise influence over the media in more subtle ways. The Hungarian government is, by far, the biggest media advertiser in the country, from the national lottery to public transport. Kim Lane Scheppele, a professor at Princeton University who has written extensively about constitutional reform and media freedom in Hungary, refers to the 'Lucky Joker rule', a reference to one of the country's most popular lottery games. By publishing advertisements in only Fidesz-friendly media, the government 'communicate[s] where it is permissible for advertisers to advertise' – in other words, it exerts pressure on all those companies that wish to win government contracts or avoid expensive tax audits. The government is therefore able to steer private advertising in the direction of those media outlets that are the least critical of it, leaving the opposition press scrounging for advertising revenue.

Peter Molnar was a classmate of Viktor Orban's and a founding member of Fidesz. He left the party in the early 1990s when it lurched from the liberal centre to the nationalist right. The new media law is a betrayal of a long lost liberal tradition, he says, referring to the 12 demands that revolutionaries proposed to the Hapsburg Empire in 1848. 'The text started with, "What does the Hungarian nation wish?"' Molnar says. 'And guess what the first point was about? Freedom of the press and no censorship.' Fidesz and the reigning Hungarian right prefer to emphasise traditional symbols of nationalism – the crown of St Stephen, Christianity, the plight of Hungarian minorities dispersed in neighbouring countries; Molnar says that freedom of thought and conscience, no less prominent in Hungarian history, are being undermined. 'With a healthy respect for facts, we just have to acknowledge, that's the tradition of Hungary. Being Hungarian means being proud of that sentence. Being committed to that sentence, to that value.'

The media law and increasingly nationalist political atmosphere in Hungary has convinced some in the West that more serious steps should be taken in response. Former American Ambassador to Hungary Mark Palmer, Johns Hopkins University Professor Charles Gati, and Hungarian author Miklos Haraszti have suggested that Radio Free Europe/Radio Liberty should resume Hungarian-language broadcasts into the country, which it ceased in 1993 shortly after the fall of communism. Budget cuts to American international broadcasting, not to mention how such a provocative move might affect US-Hungarian bilateral relations, make that prospect unlikely.

The new media law is a betrayal of a long lost tradition

Predictably, given the harsh fines that the new media authority can impose, many Hungarian journalists have complained of the law's 'chilling effect'. Yet the Hungarian independent press seems as critical of Orban and Fidesz as ever. When I pointed out the seeming contradiction to Endre Bojtar, editor of the liberal weekly *Magyar Narancs*, he responded: 'Don't mix the cause with the effect.' And he's right. Just because no journalist has (yet) been hauled off to court does not mean there is no pressure on journalists to conform. Indeed, the parlous financial state of most Hungarian independent media – and its long-time dependence on an unofficial state subsidy via the government's huge share of the advertising market – is one way in which Fidesz is slowly bringing about the demise of free media. 'It provides an opportunity for arbitrary punishment all the time,' Molnar says of the media law. 'This chilling effect creates lots of self-censorship, which is unfortunately invisible or harder to notice.'

No state can have such a law on its books and expect to call itself a liberal democracy. Even if the government doesn't opt to use such far-reaching powers, their existence poses a threat to the very notion of freedom of speech. And that threat should concern us, even if, at this point, it remains hypothetical. As Andre Bojtar says of the Fidesz government, 'They always go as far as they can, as far as the next war.' ❐

©James Kirchick
41(2): 26/30
DOI: 10.1177/0306422012448283
www.indexoncensorship.org

James Kirchick is a fellow at the Foundation for Defense of Democracies, an adjunct fellow at the Center for European Policy Analysis and a contributing editor to the *New Republic* and *World Affairs Journal*

MURDER IN DAGESTAN

Head of Dagestan's journalists' union **Ali Kamalov** fears for the future of press freedom following the murder of the country's most prominent editor

On 15 December 2011, editor and journalist Hadjimurad Kamalov was murdered in Makhachkala, the seaboard capital of Dagestan. The journalism community in Russia, and the Caucasus region as a whole, suffered a loss that could easily be equated to that of Anna Politkovskaya in 2006. He was less well known to the outside world but Dagestan, a country as large and populous as neighbouring and independent Georgia, plays a key role in the area, not least with regard to its immediate neighbour Chechnya.

Since 2005, Dagestani journalists have increasingly become targets of largely successful attempts at assassination. In March 2008, the head of broadcasting for the country, Hadji Abashilov, was shot dead. This was followed by the assassination of Telman Alishayev, author and presenter for a moderate Islamic TV channel, in September. In 2009, Malik Akhmedilov of *Khakikat* newspaper was shot dead and, in 2010, Telman Alishayev's successor, Sultan Magomedov, was assassinated.

In August 1999, the Chechen warlord Shamil Basayev and his Saudi comrade-in-arms Khattab bin Ali led a small invasion force from eastern Chechnya across the mountains into neighbouring Dagestan. This fateful event, followed by apartment bombings in subsequent months in the cities of Buinaksk (Dagestan), Volgodonsk (Southern Federal District) and, worst of all, in Moscow itself, led to the second Chechen 'war on terrorism', which began in November 1999.

In 2005, the counter-terrorist operation was declared finished in Chechnya. The small country in the North Caucasus, with a million inhabitants at the most, had paid dearly for its attempt in 1994–1996 to secure, and again in 1999–2005, to maintain a greater independence from Russia. The campaigns waged by Moscow in Chechnya could not help but affect its neighbours on the north side of the Caucasus mountain range. Ingushetia to the west was flooded by waves of displaced people and then afflicted by regular disappearances and kidnappings.

Dagestan, the largest of the seven republics, with a population of three million belonging to more than 30 different ethnic groups, has faced growing violence and instability. Basayev, Khattab and their forces were driven out but an increasingly radical youth and other local radicals began taking to the hills and the forest. If they subscribed to any clear ideology, they often proclaimed that they wanted an Islamic republic or, even, a Caliphate of all the countries in the North Caucasus, from the Black Sea to the Caspian. They engaged in persistent running battles with the local police and security forces, who themselves lost hundreds of men. Unlike Chechnya, military and police units from all over the Russian Federation have not yet been drafted in to 'help' the local authorities cope with the terrorist threat. This constant possibility remains a nightmare scenario for Dagestanis.

Hadjimurad's uncle, journalist and editor Ali Kamalov, who helped pioneer ways in which newspapers in Dagestan could survive, speaks here about free speech and the danger journalists face.

John Crowfoot

Index: Journalists continue to be killed for their work; more than ten have been murdered there since 2005. Can you tell us more about what it's like to be a journalist in Dagestan today and about the cultural, social and political climate?

Ali Kamalov: In Dagestan today, it is not only journalists that are attacked or killed. Lawyers and judges are targeted as well.

There are divisions within society. Over the past 20 years a relatively small group of people have grown rich, leaving many others impoverished and increasingly resentful. There is an ongoing struggle between different clans to divide up positions of power and authority. When journalists write about these tensions and conflicts they find themselves caught in between.

A further division is a religious one. The country is 99 per cent Muslim. State authorities in Dagestan, particularly the law enforcement agencies, have done their best to increase animosity. If people do not think like our rulers (and in Dagestan, religious leaders are close to the government) the police persecute them.

Journalists in Dagestan today act as human rights defenders. They are opposed above all to disregard for the law. They act as the people's lawyers. My nephew set up *Chernovik* in 2003 as a publication that would perform that role. *Chernovik* was a phenomenal success. Within 18 months, it had become the most popular newspaper in Dagestan. It began campaigning, not against a particular individual or on a single issue, but against shortcomings in the judicial system and the republic's law enforcement agencies. This was my nephew's achievement – the Russian political analyst Maxim Shevchenko described him as the 'Martin Luther King of the Caucasus'.

Index: Russian journalist Julia Latynina stated that Hadjimurad's death will severely restrict access to reliable information about the North Caucasus. What will be his legacy, and how is the newspaper coping without him?

Ali Kamalov: Hadjimurad was universally trusted. Prosecutors and judges feared him. Officials respected and feared him. All were reluctant to debate with him on television. The most intimidating of our ministers and prosecutors would ask me to intercede and help them restore good relations with him.

The current president of the republic became friendly with him and suggested that Hadjimurad might become a minister in Dagestan or run a major region within the country. My nephew replied: 'I am not joining the administration. If I do so I will have to abandon the newspaper and I am not prepared to do that.'

Hadjimurad demonstrated that one person can alter the way people think. Those who had not wanted to raise certain subjects in the press started to speak out when they saw what he was saying. Since his death people have again begun to fall silent. Hadjimurad would sign articles written by others to shield them from reprisals.

During the 1990s he was a college lecturer. I invited him and his two brothers to join me at our newspaper, *Khakikat* (Truth), so they would know what it means to be a journalist. He then moved to the *Novoe delo*

newspaper. It's a tabloid daily with universal appeal and, at that time, Dagestan's favourite newspaper. Hadjimurad was deputy chief editor and ran it, although he always remained in the background.

Next he set up the Free Word Institute, which was both a law firm and an institute for social analysis. Finally he started *Chernovik*, which means 'Rough Draft'. Its title comes from US publisher Philip Graham's dictum, 'a newspaper is the first draft of history'. At first the new daily ran on enthusiasm, but in time Hadjimurad's law firm and consultancy provided the income to support it. The newspaper, now headed by Hadjimurad's younger brother Magdi-Magomed, continues. But we must consider the future. There are probably people in Dagestan who want to see the paper close. Others would like to cash in on its wide appeal. For political reasons or to make money, that's why people want to own papers. Currently *Chernovik* is the only newspaper in Dagestan that pays its way.

To be frank, the newspaper lacks its former thrust and self-confidence. The president of the republic offered some funding. That means we are selling out and that society in Dagestan is not yet capable of defending the things it values.

Index: A few years back journalist and rights activist Fatima Tlisova reported that not only was she being followed around in Nalchik (Kabardino-Balkaria), but that also her children were subject to surveillance. Do similar things go on in Dagestan?

Ali Kamalov: Of course, there are threats and harassment; this is particularly the case when someone begins to expose the misdeeds of our law enforcement agencies. That explains why journalists have been murdered.

Chernovik defended anyone who was genuinely the victim of surveillance and harassment, whether they were rich or poor. Hadjimurad often used to say he was accused of being a Wahhabi. 'Yes, I'm a Wahhabi', he would say. 'I admit it. Yes, I'm a bandit, I admit it. Yes, I'm an extremist. Here, put on the cuffs, take me to jail and, if you can prove that I'm any of these things, punish me. You must not punish anyone, however, without an investigation and a trial.' Hadjimurad used to interrupt his phone conversations and say, 'Take good note of this, I'm saying this for your benefit' – addressing those whom he knew to be tapping his phone. They searched Hadjimurad's apartment, they searched my home. We were publicly denounced as extremists.

Index: Are there signs his murder is being properly investigated?

Hadjimurad Kamalov at a demonstration against law enforcement officials, 29 August 2008
Credit: Sergey Rasulov/RIA Novosti

Ali Kamalov: Authorities assure me that the investigation is making progress. I'm not convinced. After Hadji Abashilov, the director of state television, was murdered in March 2008, they carried out an investigation, arrested two lads and put them trial. The case collapsed and no verdict was reached. *Chernovik* could always defend itself in court. One entire issue, for example, exposed staff at the state prosecution service as liars and cheats. It was quite specific in its allegations and challenged the prosecution service to go to court and disprove what the newspaper said. After Hadjimurad raised the standard in this way, people began to feel more confident. The courts re-examined their own behaviour and a great many judges were dismissed. Ordinary people began feeling that the judicial system could reach fair verdicts.

Index: Who do you think killed Hadjimurad? What's the general feeling?

Ali Kamalov: There are different stories. Some say that a high-profile case like the murder of Hadjimurad was needed in the run-up to this year's Russian presidential elections. The security services wanted to unsettle people and set them against each other. The result, though, was an enormous demonstration at his funeral on a scale that Dagestan has not seen before.

Following the murder of a fellow journalist in 2008, Hadjimurad addressed a big rally and called for the Minister of Internal Affairs to resign. The response was a circular distributed within the Ministry, as we learned by chance, saying that I was shielding and supporting extremists. The brains behind this group of extremists was Hadjimurad, the note said, and it listed 27 individuals who supposedly had met at the Journalists' Club in Makhachkala with the aim of overthrowing the government. Since then two on that list have been murdered: Malik Akhmedilov, my deputy at *Khakikat*, in 2009; and Hadjimurad.

Following Hadjmurad's murder there were calls to hold protest rallies. We set up a public commission, which I myself headed, and I spoke out against such gatherings. It would have been easy to call 30,000 to 50,000 of our young people out on the streets. But this would make it all too easy to for provocateurs to create an incident that could quickly escalate, causing bloodshed. I was alarmed at the prospect.

Index: Are there journalists in jail in Dagestan?

Ali Kamalov: Not one journalist in Dagestan has been convicted and sent to prison. Instead opponents use threats, beatings and murders. I myself was attacked, on 16 May 1996, in the stairwell entrance to our apartment building, by three men. They hit me over the head and stabbed me three times in the heart. Fortunately I did not lose consciousness; otherwise, I would have quickly bled to death.

Journalists are killed with guns, mortars or explosives planted underneath their cars. Most of the killings take place in the centre of the capital, Makhachkala. In many cases the murders take place in broad daylight with traffic police and other policemen standing nearby – and yet the perpetrators are not caught. This raises the suspicion that the killers may be linked to the security services, Special Forces, the judicial system and law enforcement officials.

Hadjimurad and I often discussed the likelihood that he might be killed. Others told me: 'You must protect and defend your nephew.' He carried a gun for a while. There were times when he had bodyguards and travelled in an armour-plated vehicle. He tried to avoid going to places that were very busy. He always said: 'If they've decided to kill me, they'll succeed.'

There are all kinds of ways they could have organised his murder. Some ignorant young man may have accepted money to do the job, but the decision was taken at a high level. My nephew stirred the hostility of many powerful people in Dagestan. ❑

Translated by John Crowfoot

©John Crowfoot
41(2): 31/37
DOI: 10.1177/0306422012448593
www.indexoncensorship.org

John Crowfoot lived and worked in Moscow from 1986 to 1999. He compiled, translated and edited *A Dirty War: A Russian Reporter in Chechnya*, Anna Politkovksaya's first book in English (Harvill Press)

TIGHT SPOT

Greece's continuing economic crisis has resulted in renewed hostility towards the media. **Matthaios Tsimitakis** reports

On the night of 4 April 2012, president of the Greek Union of Photojournalists Marios Lolos attended a demonstration at Syntagma Square in Athens. An experienced photographer who had reported from war zones including Bosnia, Kosovo and the Middle East, he planned to cover the rally to mark the funeral of Dimitris Christoulas, a pensioner who had committed suicide in front of the Greek parliament a couple of days before. Prior to the suicide, the political agenda in Greece had focused mainly on security issues and racism, ignited by the government's plans to control illegal immigration through the creation of closed detention centres. But Christoulas's suicide, seen as a political act of protest against the government's austerity measures, drove attention back to the economic crisis and its severe social and political repercussions. What nobody – and certainly not Lolos – expected was that it would also trigger brutal behaviour among the city's police.

The crowd had dispersed, said Lolos, and there were only about 20 journalists left when police started using their riot shields against them. 'I started yelling, "Calm down, why are you pushing us?,"' Lolos recalls. 'Why are you asking?', a police officer responded. Lolos told the officer who he was

A photographer tries to escape damage from a petrol bomb while covering riots near parliament, Athens,
23 February 2011
Credit: Yiorgos Karahalis/Reuters

and that the journalists were simply doing their jobs. 'We have orders to evict the square,' the policeman told Lolos. 'I told him that this reminded me of authoritarian tactics. He replied that if it were so, I wouldn't even be there. As I was walking away, all of a sudden, I felt something hitting me on the head.'

Lolos was not just hit with a baton, but with the hard side of its handle, according to doctors – they also believed that the attack was inflicted with the deliberate intention of causing him serious harm. His skull bone was pushed a centimetre into his head and caused trauma to his brain. He survived death by just a millimetre but now struggles with partial paralysis. When he found out what had happened to him, he couldn't bear it. 'I survived wars to end up with paralysis in my own country,' he said, with desperation in his voice.

For the government, this was an isolated event in an otherwise democratic country. Yet there have been several incidents of police harassment against journalists during the last year. In 2011, Greece ranked 71 in the Reporters sans Frontières index of media freedom after having ranked 38 in 2008. In summer 2011, another journalist, Manolis Kypreos, was left deaf when riot police threw a stun grenade, which exploded next to his feet; the case was highlighted in an Amnesty International campaign. Reporting from the streets of Athens has been compared to reporting from a humanitarian crisis or even a war zone. Journalists, photographers and video producers are often trapped behind lines of riot police, facing hostility from protesters as well as harassment by police. This clampdown is a visible manifestation of a much deeper change in society, with direct impact on the quality of free speech in the country. Public debate has become fragmented and polarised, with extreme views splitting the population.

Behind the spectacular scenes of Athens in flames, there is a vacuum of understanding as to how these events have come about and why the media itself is part of the problem. The Greek public is unable to grasp journalists' frustration and reporters are in turn unable to inform the public in any depth because they can't gain full access to breaking stories. 'Our pictures prove that Greek police use excessive force against protesters,' says Marios Lolos. 'During the riots of December 2008, they were used as evidence to support the innocence of young people who were accused of vandalism against property or the police.' Since then, he says, journalists have been 'systematically harassed by the police' and discouraged from approaching officers when reporting on incidents. Gathering accurate information has become problematic.

Before 2008, it was equally impossible to report from a demonstration or a strike while carrying a professional camera because of hostility from the crowd. The media were associated with surveillance and discipline, linking them to the police. On several occasions in the 1990s, close-up photographs of people involved in unlawful activities at large demonstrations appeared in national newspapers and on television. Journalists were not welcome at any radical social activity. The slogan often heard on rallies was: 'Bums, pimps, journalists!' Some members of the media retreated behind the police and some relied on lazy stereotypes when describing the crowds, among them the 'hooded youth', 'anarchist', 'hooligans', 'vandals' – shady caricatures that took on the significance of the 'mujahideen' or 'terrorists' in local media.

As Marios Lolos points out, the big shift in Greece happened in 2008, when widespread rioting broke out in Athens. Citizen journalists found the field wide open and simply walked in, posting news online, reporting from behind the barricades and criticising the mainstream media. Photojournalists were the first to respond to the trend by making their photographs available to anyone who needed them. Mainstream media reacted by trying to uphold the status quo, perpetuating popular narratives that had dominated coverage of previous demonstrations. Even so, it was clear that, from then on, 'truth' would not belong exclusively to established institutions such as governmental agencies and big media companies. Now it was more likely to be an open social process.

In this context, 'truth' represented a contest between different interpretations of social, economic and political conditions. In Greece these conditions are determined to a great extent by corruption, political nepotism and *diaploki* – the intertwining interests of businessmen, the media and politicians. It is within this framework that the Greek media industry developed, along with deliberate unlawfulness, deregulation and economic failures. In 1988, Greece had a population of ten million people and 450 media companies. In 2008, the population had risen by a million people and media companies numbered 2,500.

Many of these companies operated without a licence and under the protection of influential politicians from the two main parties, with negative results for their image – many were seen as fronts for illegal business. Censorship and self-censorship were, and still are, common practice. The economic crisis has compounded the situation so that an open war has been declared upon journalists' rights, from wages and social security to the right to free speech. Over the past two years, more than 30 per cent of the country's media workers have lost their jobs; on average, the whole of the work force has suffered a 25 per cent reduction in wages, creating a climate of fear within the industry. Union members working for big media companies have also lost their jobs and been given the excuse that the redundancies are a result of the economic crisis. Self-censorship is now the only way to survive in the media, given that it has demonstrated its widespread support for austerity measures and the policies of the International Monetary Fund and the European Union, despite opinion polls that suggest the wider population does not agree. Oppositional voices from the left are marginalised and weaker, independent newspapers face bankruptcy. Unemployed journalists have started cooperatives that support small-scale projects like news magazines or online initiatives where production costs are minimal – but so is recognition.

In a recent interview with al Jazeera, the president of the Athenian Association of Journalists (ESIEA) Dimitris Trimis spoke of the enormous influence political commentary in the mainstream media has upon the population. During the demonstrations against the austerity measures in 2011 and prior to parliament voting on the issue, the Greek media were 'systematically twisting reality' and spreading misinformation, adding that it downplayed the numbers of protesters and misrepresented their demands. Reporting focused on property damage and reduced the story to a simple 'good police' versus 'bad protesters' scenario. Dimitris Trimis is the first unemployed president in the union's 100-year history. He lost his job after *Eleftherotypia*, a symbol of the centre-left and one of the biggest papers in the country, went into bankruptcy.

Nowadays, every time there's a protest in Athens, a well-planned strategy must be adopted in order to follow and report on it. In typical fashion, television crews remain behind police lines and on rooftops in 'surveillance' positions, photojournalists position themselves between protesters and police, while citizen journalists and small media representatives choose to mix with demonstrators in an attempt to document incidents in detail.

Thanks to the internet, the public now has access to a larger number of voices and opinions, a kind of polyphony that strengthens and deepens the critical debate so crucial to a thriving democracy. But in the current crisis, where austerity has led to despair and despair has led to tension, a degree of authoritarianism has taken hold, resulting in a cacophony. Everyone shouts at everyone and communication has broken down.

This hostile environment was evident in the elections on 6 May. There were representatives from 32 parties on the ballot, resulting in widespread rejection of the two main parties and no clear winners. In some cases, the power struggle between the media and politicians has been all too apparent. During a press conference, the nationalist, neo-Nazi Golden Dawn party, which won 21 seats, demanded that journalists stand as a mark of respect when the party leader Nikos Mihaloliakos entered the room. Instead, many journalists chose to leave. Amidst this confusion and noise, where the very fabric of Greek society is being broken down, in a state of widespread anxiety, poverty and democratic malfunctions, something seems to be lost from the very essence of free speech. ❒

©Matthaios Tsimitakis
41(2): 38/42
DOI: 10.1177/0306422012448785
www.indexoncensorship.org

Matthaios Tsimitakis is a freelance journalist based in Athens

SPORT ON TRIAL

Should sport make way for human rights?

Olympic Stadium, East London, 27 October 2010
Credit: Suzanne Plunkett/Reuters

SPORTING TRIALS

Should sport give as much regard to human rights as athletic prowess? **Mihir Bose** considers a troubled relationship with ethics

On the evening of 13 July 2001, as Beijing held a press conference in Moscow to celebrate securing the 2008 Olympics, they had an unexpected visitor: François Carrard, the Swiss lawyer who was executive director of the International Olympic Committee (IOC). Normally on such occasions the IOC keeps its distance and lets the victorious city have its moment in the sun. But Carrard felt he had to address the media on the human rights issue.

In the lead-up to the vote, Beijing's rivals, in particular Toronto and Paris, had made much of China's human rights record. As the members gathered, some 50 protesters assembled outside chanting 'Free Tibet'. The Russian police, some wearing riot gear, broke up the protest and six people were seen being taken away in a waiting bus after demonstrators tried to unfurl three banners on the Moscow River embankment, opposite the World Trade Centre where the IOC was meeting. There were reports of 12 arrests.

The IOC had so far refused to discuss human rights, arguing that it was only concerned with making a decision about sport. Nor was the issue addressed by the Evaluation Commission that visited the bid cities and whose assessment formed the basis of the IOC members' decision. The report of the commission was crucial as, following the revelation of the 1998 Salt Lake City corruption scandal in which IOC members were accused of taking bribes, they were subsequently barred from visiting bid cities. Just before the vote for the 2008 Games, Hein Verbruggen, the Dutch chairman of the Evaluation Commission, summarised to his fellow members the various potential risk factors of the bidding cities. But he did not mention human rights.

Beijing did face a question on human rights during its presentation. But this was delivered in such a roundabout way that only seasoned IOC observers could have understood it. Roland Baar, a rower from Germany, raised the ethical issue of playing beach volleyball in Tiananmen Square. Beijing had proposed this idea, but it had been shelved after objections from the Evaluation Commission that it was not a suitable venue. Baar was so circumspect that he did not even utter the words 'Tiananmen Square', lest it offend the Chinese.

But now Carrard felt free to talk about human rights. At the press conference, apologising profusely for intervening at the Chinese party, he revealed, 'On human rights we had two choices – a decision we close the door and that is a hugely respectable decision. The other way is to bet on openness. We bet that in seven years' time the interactions, the progress and the development will be such that human rights can be improved.'

Long before the Beijing Olympics was staged it was clear that this was an impossible bet, and in the end Jacque Rogge, who was elected president of the IOC a few days after the vote in Moscow, made it clear that it was no business of the committee to monitor China's moral development. Indeed, Rogge confessed that the IOC neither had the power nor the ability to do anything on human rights. The result: China rode out the protests that accompanied the Games, in particular the ones that marked the torch relay. China, as it had always planned, used the Games to show they could take the Olympics, a western invention, and do it better. By the end of it, IOC members were applauding the Games as China's giant coming-out party and declaring the bar had been raised to such an extent that other countries would struggle to match it. All talk of human rights and opening up the country had vanished.

The fact was that the Games went to Beijing not because the Olympic movement thought it could change China, but because of wider geopolitical considerations. The overwhelming view of IOC members was that the Games had to go to the most populous country in the world. China had been a good Olympic member. Whatever its human rights record, there was no Olympic reason to refuse the bid. There was also a fear that Beijing, having failed in 1993 when it lost to Sydney by two votes, might walk out of the Olympics if China did not succeed this time.

Police arrest a Tibetan protester near the venue of the Olympic torch relay, New Delhi, India, 17 April 2008
Credit: Reuters

There was a dominant view in the Olympic movement that, with the collapse of the Soviet Union, a strong China was needed to balance the all-powerful Americans. Ivan Slavkov, the IOC member from Bulgaria – later expelled from the movement in 2005 when he was caught by an undercover reporter saying he would take bribes in exchange for votes – said at the time: 'We need China to act as a check on the US. The US is the only superpower. It dominates everything, including the Olympics and the medal tables. China is coming up fast and, by giving the Games to them, we can make sure they develop in the right direction.'

The IOC's dance round the issue of human rights over the decades illustrates a wider problem for all sports organisations faced with such ethical concerns. The classic example of this was the 1936 Berlin Olympics. The award of the Games to Berlin was intended to symbolise the re-admission of a peaceful, democratic Germany to the family of nations after the horrors of the First World War. By a supreme irony, the Games have gone down in history as a triumph of Nazi propaganda. As the official *Olympic-Zeitung* proudly asked on 19 August 1936: 'Do we have to point out that the great victor at the Olympic Games is Adolf Hitler?'

The 1936 Olympics, which left us the legacy of the torch relay, offers a template for the use of sport for ulterior purposes with its extraordinary mixture of opportunism, improvisation and attention to detail in the Nazi preparations for the Games. But Hitler could not have fulfilled his agenda to show how normal his regime was if leaders of international sport had not played into his hands, with their willingness to believe dishonest public assurances and to accept gestures and symbols rather than look at reality.

Since then, sports leaders have often looked the other way when major sporting events are held against a background of state violence, in countries whose repressive regimes seek to present themselves as open societies to the outside world. The list includes rebel South African cricket tours of the apartheid era, financed by tax concessions by the white regime, the 1968 Mexico Olympics, the Ali-Foreman fight in 1974 in a Zaire ruled by the brutal and corrupt despot Mobutu Sese Seko, and the 1978 World Cup in Argentina, organised by a junta which, even then, was embarking on a massive pro-gramme of killing people opposed to the regime.

Back in 1851, when Prince Albert wished to advertise the might of Queen Victoria's realm he held a Great Exhibition – essentially a trade fair displaying the works of industry of all nations. There was culture in the form of Charlotte Bronte, Lewis Carroll and George Eliot, but no sport.

Today, sporting events have come to replace trade expos as a symbol of national success. Nelson Mandela used the power of sport, particularly rugby, to woo the whites, and felt that the rainbow nation had arrived when in 2010 it became the first African country to stage the football World Cup. In Copenhagen in 2009, President Lula of Brazil shed tears after Rio won the right to stage the 2016 Olympics. 'Everybody talks of Brazil as the coun-try of tomorrow,' he said. 'Here in Copenhagen tomorrow has arrived.' His pleasure was all the greater as Rio had beaten Barack Obama's Chicago, despite the fact that the most powerful man in the world made a personal plea to the IOC.

But the problem for sport is that, unlike expos, it carries a moral dimen-sion. It is interesting to note that Beijing's rivals made much of this distinction. Claude Bébéar, president of the Paris bid, made it clear he would have no problems with a Chinese city hosting an expo, but not the Olympics. Giving China the Games, he argued, would indicate moral approval for the regime.

Rudolf Hess and Adolf Hitler in the stands at the opening ceremony of the 1936 Berlin Olympics
Credit: Ullstein Bild/akg-images

The idea that sport had universal significance emerged only in the 19th century as the rules for modern sports were being formulated. In his fictional novel *Tom Brown's Schooldays*, Thomas Hughes presented his headmaster at Rugby, Thomas Arnold, as a sporting guru. His message, said Hughes, was that sport could reach out beyond the playing fields more effectively than any other form of human activity. Indeed, sport could shape society for the greater good.

The headmaster of Hughes's book was an invention – the real life Arnold had no interest in sport. But the idea proved so powerful that it seduced a French baron, Pierre de Coubertin, who came to Rugby to worship at Arnold's shrine and used his principles to revive the Olympics, setting it a high political goal. As he put it: 'It is clear the telegraph, railways, the telephone, the passionate research in science, congresses and exhibitions have done more for peace than any treaty or diplomatic convention. Well, I hope that athletics will do even more … let us export runners and fencers; there is a free trade of the future, and on the day when it is introduced within the walls of old Europe the cause of peace would have received a new and mighty stay.'

Modern sport is essentially the marriage of Hughes's big idea in the private realm – that sport develops character – with Coubertin's big idea in the public realm – that sport can transmit values within and between nations through regular international competition.

The problem arises when sport collides with political reality, as it did in the wake of the Arab spring. As millions rose up in the Arab world last year to challenge and even change their despotic rulers, in Bahrain the desire for freedom came into conflict with modern sport. In the picturesque words of the *Daily Mail's* Martin Samuel, the result of 'little brown people' wanting freedom meant 'the next thing you know is there is one less place for rich white guys to race cars'.

Formula One's first Grand Prix of the season was due to take place in Bahrain in March, just weeks after the kingdom had been engulfed by protesters demanding more freedom. There had been highly publicised protests at the main Pearl Roundabout in the financial district of Manama with some 31 protesters killed. Armoured cars, including Saudi troops and forces from Qatar and UAE, had rolled into the kingdom to restore order. How could a sports event take place in such a climate? And where was the moral compass of sport in even thinking it could?

The race was the dream of Crown Prince Sheikh Salman bin Hamad bin Isa al Khalifa, who had made it clear that money was no object in bringing one of the most high profile world events to his desert kingdom. The Bahrain government funded the race. The Sakhir circuit, where the Grand Prix had been run since 2004, had cost some £92m. The F1 organisers had been paid £24.6m to allow Bahrain to organise the opening race of the 2010 season, and this had risen by 60 per cent for the 2011 race. The protesters knew how dear the race was to the Crown Prince and that if they wanted to wring political concessions from him, they had to hit at his beloved sport.

However, the F1 organisers of the race did not seem to understand the moral questions involved. Neither FIA, the governing body, nor Bernie Ecclestone – the F1 rights holder – wanted to put their heads above the parapet. Their reluctance, it was assumed, was due to the fear that if they cancelled the race they would stand to lose £37m in rights fees.

In the end, the Crown Prince himself decided the race had to be put back, hoping it could be held later in the year. His wish appeared to have been granted when, following an FIA inspection team visit, FIA's World Council unanimously agreed that the Bahrain Grand Prix would now be held

Anti-Formula One graffiti, Barbar, near Manama, Bahrain, 5 April 2012
Credit: Hamad I Mohammed/Reuters

on 30 October. The decision provoked outrage from human rights activists and race fans. Many argued that for all the talk of high values, sport was more bothered about Mammon and ended up conspiring with despots.

The FIA's judgement was further called into question when details of the inspection report emerged. Over a two-day trip, the FIA had met the minister of culture and tourism, the minister of the interior, had had lunch with the board that runs the Grand Prix, met circuit personnel and visited a shopping centre. But they had not met any of the dissidents. It was clear that the race could now not go ahead at the rescheduled date either. However, it was logistics not morality that was given as the reason for the cancellation. The new date for the race in October meant Bahrain would get India's Grand Prix schedule – the new Formula One commercial centre – and extend the calendar into December. The teams just could not cope with the pressures this would create.

The whole affair brought little credit to Formula One, least of all the highly paid drivers. Apart from Red Bull's Mark Webber, who acknowledged the moral question of sport taking place in the wake of a bloodbath, nearly all the other drivers avoided the moral issue. I could not even coax Britain's most successful F1 driver, Nigel Mansell – who has chalked up 31 race wins and the 1992 world title – to take a stand on this issue. When I asked in the middle of the crisis whether it would be morally justified to stage the Bahrain Grand Prix, Mansell replied: 'There are great people involved in Formula One who are in charge and it is up to them to speak to the power brokers of the country.'

Zayed al Zayani, the businessman appointed by the Crown Prince to run the Grand Prix, was emphatic that the press, particularly the British press, had got the human rights situation in Bahrain dreadfully wrong. His country, he argued, was not to be compared with the rest of the Arab world. Indeed it was no different to most other countries. If F1 could go to China, why not Bahrain? 'They're going to the US next year,' he said. 'What about Guantanamo? Isn't that human rights violation?' As Bernie Ecclestone had told him: 'If human rights were the criterion for F1 races, we would only have them in Belgium and Switzerland in the future.' Indeed, by not going to Bahrain, he lamented, F1 had missed out on a great chance of using the race to unite the country.

The problem here, as Max Mosley, the former head of FIA, astutely put it was: 'The Formula One world did not seem to appreciate that the government in Bahrain was about to use the Grand Prix in support of suppressing human rights.'

For all the moral high ground Formula One may like to claim, when faced with a stark ethical issue it is powerless and has to duck and dive. The same drama has played itself out again this year, with F1 facing international condemnation for holding the race in Bahrain.

Sports administrators may present themselves as the Vatican of sport, beyond the control of any authority but their own. Yet the money needed to run modern sport means they have to compromise with dubious governments and regimes. The result is that the high moral purpose of sport is sacrificed if not totally ignored. And until sport can deal with this basic contradiction, problems such as Bahrain will continue to appear. The worrying thing is that few in sport seem willing or able to deal with it. ❐

©Mihir Bose
41(2): 48/55
DOI: 10.1177/0306422012447740
www.indexoncensorship.org

Mihir Bose is the author of *The Spirit of the Game: How Sport Made the Modern World* (Constable)

Athol Fugard
Challenging the silence

*The problems created by the policy of apartheid
for the theatre in South Africa are discussed
by the playwright, actor and producer Athol
Fugard in this interview with Michael Coveney,
Assistant Editor of* Plays and Players (*November
1973*).

*Athol Fugard was in London to produce his
play* Sizwe Bansi Is Dead, *which he had written in
collaboration with the two actors taking part
in it, John Kani and Winston Ntshona, and
which has been very well received both at*
The Theatre Upstairs *in London and on its tour
of the provinces in November and December.*

**We read in the papers here that Sizwe Bansi
was hauled off the stage by the police when you
presented it in South Africa.**

We've been hauled off the stage a number of
times. Just before coming here we continually
ran into trouble in our attempts to play *Sizwe
Bansi* publicly to white audiences in South
Africa. We were stopped every time, and we
finally came to terms with that. But immediately
before we came here the play was scheduled for
four performances to a coloured audience – you
must remember that the basic racial categories
in South Africa are white (Afrikaaner), then
coloured, then black. We had long since learned
to cope with not playing publicly to white, but
we had *never* run into trouble with playing to
coloured; but, on this occasion, with two *black*
actors playing to a *coloured* audience, the police
came in about five hours before the first
performance to say that if we were to proceed,
we would be prosecuted.

**Despite that intervention, you came with the
blessing of the government. You were given
passports.**

I don't think we have the blessing of the
government, I cannot understand why we were
finally given passports, because the work we

were doing was intended only for South Africa;
and we were trying to be as courageous as
possible in that context, in indicting a social
system. On the face of it, this indictment was
given permission to be seen abroad. It may be
that our efforts come to nothing, that the
government thought, 'Well, the worst they can
do is to show it to a lot of already converted
English liberals'; or, and I incline to this feeling:
the endless traumas undergone by South Africa
in terms of the withdrawal and refusal of
passports do damage to the South African image
abroad, and I think we might have been
considered an instance where a certain value
was to be gained in granting the passport rather
than withholding it.

**To have withheld your passport would have
meant hostile publicity for them?**

Yes. I lost my passport for a period of 4½ years
and it was finally returned merely on the basis
of a very outraged public opinion in South Africa.
That period coincided with some very significant
productions of my work outside of the country.
I could never attend these productions and
because South Africans got sick and bloody
tired of reading about this I was finally granted
my passport, I think. Of course they never tell
you why a passport is withdrawn or returned;
the classic formula is ' for reasons of state
security '.

**Tell us about Serpent Players, the group who
present your latest play.**

I have a fairly adulterous relationship with
theatre in South Africa. I work with white
actors. I work with black actors. Maybe that's
why I feel tired; adultery is not easy! Serpent
Players is one of the very meaningful relationships
I've had for a long time, a group of black
actors in my home town, Port Elizabeth. It
started about ten years ago when there was a
knock on my front door, seven men walked in

BOMB PSYCHOLOGY

Celebrated playwright **Athol Fugard** explained to Michael Coveney why he opposed calls for a cultural and sports boycott of South Africa

What is your reaction to the boycott mentality prevalent among most British dramatists, and the many pressure groups here who agitate for sporting and academic boycotts of South Africa?

This is something on which for the moment I am prepared to jettison my confusion and make unequivocal statements. There was a time when managements in South Africa had the choice of playing in a 'whites only' context or going into certain venues where, under the laws still operative, the audiences and possibly even the actors could have been multi-racial. At the point when this choice was still possible I advocated, and I take the responsibility (not the credit) for initiating, the boycott. Then legislation was enacted which removed that choice, and it was then a question of (a) surrendering oneself to silence, or (b) taking on the new circumstances and audiences of whites only, blacks only, or coloureds only. I decided that I was not in favour of silence, so I changed my stand on the cultural boycott; and although I have been under pressure many times, I have no intention of changing it again. You mention the sports boycott. On this I have become increasingly irritated. Because there are many people abroad who, while agreeing with me that there should continue to enter the country a free flow of ideas (because this is in fact what the South African government would keep out), say, at the same time, let's have these ideas coming in but, for God's sake, not sportsmen! I have come to the conclusion that this distinction involves a monumental cultural conceit. I just don't know how anybody can define what is a significant act, what is a significant thought; whether Gary Sobers on a cricket pitch is more or less important than Paul Scofield in a Pinter play. That for me looks like a conceit. My view is that a boycott psychology is a bomb psychology. One solution to the South African problem is to drop a bloody great hydrogen bomb on the country, blow the whole thing to ashes and then give a lot of immigrants from somewhere else a chance of living on that bit of parched earth. I'm not interested in that. I'm interested in the survival of what I know is still there, vital and intact.

Only one or two authors here have flaunted the cultural boycott, but it would be presumptuous to condemn those who haven't. After all, you live in the middle of it, people here are trapped inside received information and act according to that and their consciences.

That's absolutely right. I've had one enormously significant encounter about the boycott, and that was with Arnold Wesker, an initial signatory to the whole boycott declaration, who found himself assailed with doubts. When we met up, about three years ago, he asked me about the situation. I would not attempt to convert anybody, that's not my job. People must care about it enough to ask me and then I will very hesitantly, and with due modesty, venture a statement on the realities. Arnold asked and it was therefore easy for me to tell him that there *are* pockets of decency, there *are* venues, there *are* groups, there *are* underground situations which, if he were to give them permission to do his work, would be the stronger for that; Arnold said that at this distance he could not possibly know that; but he agreed for his plays to be done on the condition that I, as a friend, should vet the circumstances. And if he had been in South Africa when his work was done, he would have been very proud. ❐

This is an extract from a longer interview first published in Plays and Players

©Athol Fugard
41(2): 56/58
DOI: 10.1177/0306422012447744
www.indexoncensorship.org

GAME
CONTROL

Who owns the Olympics? **Stephen Escritt** and **Martin Polley** investigate London 2012's attempt to privatise the very meaning of the Games

During London's campaign to host the 2012 Olympic Games many local businesses in East London leant their support, prominently 'backing the bid' in their shop windows. Following London's victory, scaffolding firms, minicab companies, kebab shops and convenience stores in the host boroughs of the Games changed their names: the Olympic Kebab, Olympic Cash & Carry, Olympic Skips and other variations proliferated.

However, the newly created London Organising Committee of the Olympic Games (Locog) was much less keen for small businesses to associate themselves with the Games than its predecessor had been during the fevered bidding process. The 'Olympic' businesses gradually began to receive letters from Locog threatening legal action, leading most to temper their enthusiasm and revert to their previous names.

It is not only the use of the word Olympic that prompted threats of legal action. According to Locog's brand protection guidance, combining the words Games, 2012, Two Thousand and Twelve and Twenty Twelve with gold, silver, bronze, medals, sponsor or summer could also constitute an infringement. The guidance also noted ominously that 'an association can

Olympic Kebab shop and owner, London, circa 2009–10, from Olympics *by Martyn Routledge at Open Agency. To buy a copy for £8.99, visit openthebook.com (£1 will go to Prostate Cancer Charity)*

also be created without having used one of the Listed Expressions'. Just how far Locog felt that it could control the use of language in the run-up to the Games was demonstrated last year when it threatened a commercial venture called the Great Exhibition 2012 with legal action.

At the time, a Locog spokesman told the BBC that the basis for the Great Exhibition 2012 challenge was the 'London Olympic and Paralympic Games Act 2006 [which] prevents people from creating an unauthorised association between a person, organisation, business, goods and services and the London 2012 Games'. Mathew Healey, trademark attorney at law firm Bates Wells & Braithwaite, describes the Act as: 'An extremely tough law. In effect it prevents any "unauthorised person", anyone except official sponsors such as Coca Cola or McDonald's, from doing anything that "is likely to create in the public mind an association" between the 2012 Olympics and that person, and/or their goods, services or activities.' Healey adds: 'The rights accorded to Locog are extremely broad. Many in the legal and marketing sectors believe they go beyond what is necessary to protect their legitimate interests.'

The Olympics has far greater protection in law than any other brand, and governments are quick to legislate to protect it as part of the deal to host the Games. The draconian nature of this very broadly drafted protection leads many to choose to play it safe and effectively self-police, even in the not-for-profit, cultural and educational sectors. When the 2012 Games bid was successful, much was made of the role of the Cultural Olympiad and how the UK cultural sector had its part to play. However, it was soon made known to arts organisations through various briefings and meetings that certain words would be out of bounds when it came to artistic programming and that an association would only be possible through sanctioned use of the 2012 'inspire mark', a logo awarded to a number of non-commercial organisations allowing association with the Games. Only '*incidental* use in literary or artistic works' is given as a defence against infringement of the 2006 Act.

By creating only one type of activity that can legally be called 'Olympic', the International Olympic Committee (IOC) has monopolised a word that was in general use for centuries before Pierre de Coubertin established the modern Olympic Games in 1896. As a result, events that were named after the Olympics before Coubertin's time are now seen as 'pseudo' Olympics, or as forerunners to Coubertin's version. All would be subject to legal challenge if they were conceived today.

There were Robert Dover's Games, which started in Chipping Campden in the early 17th century and were called Olimpicks by 1636, a name that has stuck. Robert Dover's Cotswold Olimpicks are still held every summer. The poets who gave this anti-puritanical romp the Olimpick name were showing off their knowledge of classical literature: bear in mind that it was William Shakespeare who first used 'Olympian' in print in modern English, in *Henry VI, Part 3*.

After Richard Chandler, an Englishman, discovered the site of ancient Olympia in 1766, a new wave of Olympic events emerged. In Hendon in 1786, for example, there was an event that was advertised as 'a burlesque imitation of the Olympic Games', with similar events in Hampstead before the century's end. More people used the name over the course of the 19th century, as a general fashion for classicism met news of the excavation of Olympia. These included sporting events, like Baron de Berenger's Olympic Festival at Chelsea's Cremorne Gardens in 1832, as well as circus acts and theatres, like the Olympic Pavilion, which opened in London's Drury Lane in 1806 for equestrian spectaculars, and was later renamed the Olympic

The president of McDonald's and International Olympic Committee president Dr Jacques Rogge (second from right) sign a contract securing McDonald's sponsorship of the Olympic Games through to 2020
Credit: Kerstin Joensson/AP Images for McDonald's

Theatre under Eliza Vestris's direction. A rare poster from Oswestry in 1834, written in a phonetic rendering of a Shropshire accent, promised 'Gim Nas Stick Xercisez, Ho-Lympic Gaymes, Hand Ethennyun Sportes'.

Then there were Pablo Fanque's Olympian Games, a touring equestrian circus act of the 1850s. The name became more sporting thanks to the successful Wenlock Olympian Games, which started in 1850 and are thriving today, as well as the Liverpool Olympic Festivals of the 1860s and the National Olympian Games, held in London in 1866 and Birmingham in 1867. Coubertin was born in 1863, and he clearly borrowed ideas and terminology from these events.

Most intriguing were the Morpeth Olympic Games, a racing and wrestling event for miners and quarrymen that started in the Northumberland town in the 1870s. It survived, cash prizes and betting culture intact, until 1958. Then, of course, there was Blackburn Olympic FC, the first working-class team

Locog's guidance on 'protected' words, from 'Brand protection',
London 2012's UK statutory marketing rights, April 2010

Flowchart summarising OSPA

(This flowchart reflects the provisions of the Olympic Symbol etc (Protection) Act 1995 (as amended).)

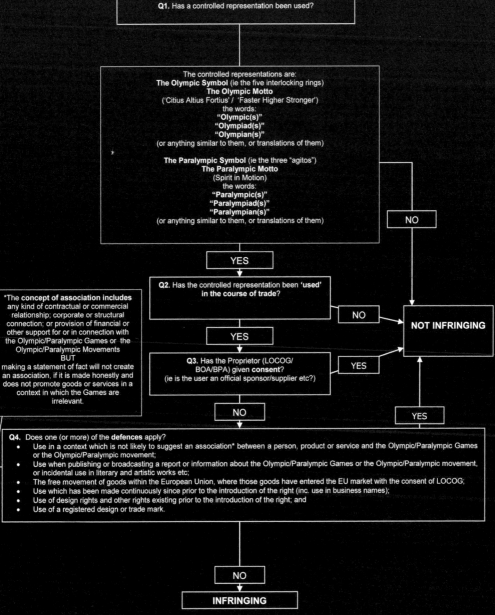

Q1. Has a controlled representation been used?

The controlled representations are:
The Olympic Symbol (ie the five interlocking rings)
The Olympic Motto
('Citius Altius Fortius' / 'Faster Higher Stronger')
the words:
"Olympic(s)"
"Olympiad(s)"
"Olympian(s)"
(or anything similar to them, or translations of them)

The Paralympic Symbol (ie the three "agitos")
The Paralympic Motto
(Spirit in Motion)
the words:
"Paralympic(s)"
"Paralympiad(s)"
"Paralympian(s)"
(or anything similar to them, or translations of them)

NO

YES

Q2. Has the controlled representation been 'used' in the course of trade?

*The **concept of association includes** any kind of contractual or commercial relationship; corporate or structural connection; or provision of financial or other support for or in connection with the Olympic/Paralympic Games or the Olympic/Paralympic Movements BUT making a statement of fact will not create an association, if it is made honestly and does not promote goods or services in a context in which the Games are irrelevant.

NO

YES

NOT INFRINGING

Q3. Has the Proprietor (LOCOG/ BOA/BPA) given **consent**? (ie is the user an official sponsor/supplier etc?)

YES

NO

YES

Q4. Does one (or more) of the **defences** apply?
- Use in a context which is not likely to suggest an association* between a person, product or service and the Olympic/Paralympic Games or the Olympic/Paralympic movement;
- Use when publishing or broadcasting a report or information about the Olympic/Paralympic Games or the Olympic/Paralympic movement, or incidental use in literary and artistic works etc;
- The free movement of goods within the European Union, where those goods have entered the EU market with the consent of LOCOG;
- Use which has been made continuously since prior to the introduction of the right (inc. use in business names);
- Use of design rights and other rights existing prior to the introduction of the right; and
- Use of a registered design or trade mark.

NO

INFRINGING

This document provides LOCOG's interpretation of its statutory rights only and is not a substitute for legal advice. If you think you may have infringed our rights, or you are proposing to do something which you think may infringe our rights, we recommend that you seek independent legal advice.   V30.04.10

Helms Bakeries, 16 March 2005. The bakeries catered to the 1932 Los Angeles Olympics
Credit: Jim Sedgwick/blogging.la

to win the FA Cup with their 1883 triumph over Old Etonians. The name continued to have an appeal outside sport, as witness the renaming of the National Agricultural Hall in Kensington as Olympia in 1886, and the naming of *Titanic*'s sister ship *RMS Olympic* in 1910.

So Coubertin was not the first to call his event Olympic. He was working in a long tradition, one informed by an interest in classical history, and by a desire to add lustre to modern events by naming them after the famous games of ancient Greece. And while Coubertin attempted to close off alternative, non-sporting meanings early on in the IOC's history, in 1910 he acknowledged the fact that the name could not be monopolised: 'The term is in the public domain. If you are not afraid of looking ridiculous, and if your efforts are considerable enough to be compared to what goes into organising a standard Olympiad, go ahead and use it. No one has the right to prevent you from doing so.'

The fact that the Morpeth Olympic Games survived under that name until 1958, untroubled by cease-and-desist letters from the IOC's lawyers, shows the longevity of tolerated alternatives. Ironically, during the first half of the 20th century Olympic organisers and officials seemed quaintly naive about language and branding. According to Professor Alan Tomlinson of Brighton University, in a paper about the commercialisation of the Olympics, 'entrepreneurial operators from outside the IOC were the ones to see the potential of the commercialisation process'. Helms Bakeries of Los Angeles, founded in 1931, was contracted to supply the Olympic Village at the Olympics in LA in 1932. Founder Paul H Helms duly registered the marks of the Olympics in all the US states, including the five rings and the word 'Olympic', something neither the IOC nor any other connected organisation had ever thought to do. Helms Olympic Bread continued as a brand, until its founder generously gave up the rights in the 1950s, allowing the IOC to lay the foundations for its own eventual stranglehold on Olympic language.

It was in the 1980s, as income from traditional sources began to fall and the Olympics became more expensive to stage, that the IOC began to sell the brand to commercial sponsors. When the 1984 Los Angeles Olympics were audited and found to have made a surplus of $222m, a new era of commercialisation and control was born. As far as using the word Olympic is concerned, Coubertin's assurance has been conveniently brushed aside, offering little protection to the owner of the former Olympic Kebab shop in Hackney Wick contemplating whether his business would have really undermined McDonald's role as 'official restaurant of the Olympic movement'. ❏

©Stephen Escritt and Martin Polley
41(2): 59/65
DOI: 10.1177/0306422012447742
www.indexoncensorship.org

Stephen Escritt is a partner at Counterculture and works with a range of arts and cultural organisations
Martin Polley is a sports historian, author, broadcaster and senior lecturer in sport at the University of Southampton. Their exhibition *Politics & Olympics, Ideals and Realities* runs from May Day until the close of the Paralympic Games in September at the Free Word Centre in London

*Dennis Spur's Fantastic Sausage Factory shop in Dorset has been ordered
to remove a sign featuring Olympics rings made out of sausages*
Credit: Geoff Moore/Rex Features

BAD SPORT

Natalie Haynes gets to grips with the rules and
regs policing the brand of the London Games

As a general rule, when a private company says that its ruthlessly tight protection against copyright infringement is for public benefit, my skin starts to itch. Sometimes at least you can understand the rationale: if we all stop buying music and pinch it off the internet, there will undoubtedly be fewer musicians making enough money to stay in the music-making business, and that would be rotten. The charts will be packed out with trust-fund babies and bankers having a mid-life crisis (in my house, we call them U2).

But the way to stop this happening is probably not to threaten anyone who's ever had broadband and an iPod with a lengthy jail sentence and a bazillion dollar fine, because that is simply antagonistic, and makes them forget how much they like musicians in their dislike of record companies. And while you're at it, you remind the rest of us that we hate global corporations too.

The same is true of what appears to be the most heavily copyrighted event the world has ever seen: the 2012 Olympics. Now, you may have been thinking that Locog, the London Olympic organisers, have been playing a long game, with their piss-poor logo, weirdly condomic mascots and vile 80s' graffiti font. We scoffed as each one was released, little realising that this was surely the strongest protection against counterfeit items: who could possibly want to fake something so intrinsically crappy?

Nonetheless, Locog takes its copyright position very seriously. So seriously, in fact, that it has released a 61-page document of guidelines to explain how we can all not infringe their rights. They begin by stating that they hope all the information given will be used in good faith, which makes it all the odder that they let smart-arse journalists anywhere near it. While each page concludes with a footer stating that it is no substitute for legal advice, it does offer two separate flowcharts, and some Olympic background.

Given how much of the Olympic background is really quite dodgy and racist, I was hoping for a good read. But there is no mention of the Nazi background of the Olympic torch (the torch relay first took place in Berlin, 1936, and has nothing to do with ancient Greece, beyond the fact that Hitler liked to associate himself with the ancient world, because it seemed to validate him).

There's also no mention of the dubious colour-scheme origins of the Olympic rings, which were once meant to symbolise directly the continents involved: blue for Europe, green for Australia (nice and uncontroversial), red for America (oh, like the native Americans? Wait, this is less controversial, right?), yellow for Asia (now, hang on) and black for Africa (okey dokey, then). The executive committee of the International Olympic Committee removed the paragraph explaining this from its booklet in 1951. But again, sadly no mention in the Olympic background info this year.

What they do mention is how many, many ways you could breach the Olympic copyright, even if you weren't trying. 'Controlled phrases', in Locog parlance, include 'Games, two thousand and twelve, 2012, and twenty twelve' (that's list A), and 'Gold, silver, bronze, London, medals, sponsors and summer' (that's list B). Combining words from either or both lists might give rise to a 'Listed expression', which is another thing you're not supposed to be doing.

Don't feel that Orwell has descended, however. Locog makes exceptions (possibly – they're listed as 'defences', just so you know you're in the wrong before you start). Gratifyingly, you can use words associated with the Olympics if it's perfectly clear you aren't trying to have anything to do with them. So, to quote their example, an antique store could advertise an 'Original Marble Olympian Statue, circa 500 BC', and that would probably be fine.

What, you may wonder, is the sound of the Olympics?

And if you have a company name which sounds a bit Olympicky, that's okay too, so long as you existed before the Olympics and don't pretend that you have anything to do with them. The example they give for this is my favourite bit of the whole document (page 17, in case you were thinking I stopped early). They suggest that if a pen manufacturer had trademarked the name 'Olympens' that would probably be okay. Seriously? Olympens? Suddenly, the amazing rubbishness of brand names that contestants on *The Apprentice* come up with all makes sense. Was Olympens really the best anyone could come up with? They couldn't put aside four more seconds and invent a company that sells ice picks for climbing in Greek mountains?

But it's not just the logos of the Olympics, or words that might loosely have anything to do with them, which are subject to these controls. Just to clarify: 'An infringing association can be created by the use of *any* "representation". This may be an image, graphic design, sound, or word (spoken or written) etc' (their emphasis). What, you may be wondering, is the sound of the Olympics? The gentle flow of tenners as they sink into an open drain?

Locog are keen to point out, as I said back at the start, that they are doing all of this for our benefit. If their sponsors aren't protected, then they might pull out. And if they do that, there will be a big fat chasm in the Olympics budget, and you and I will be left with the bill.

At no point does it seem to have occurred to them, in their mesmerising arrogance, that every London council tax payer is also one of their sponsors, and has been for years. It also hasn't occurred to them that they could always have simply spent less on their massive school sports day, instead of tanking billions and then telling us we should count ourselves lucky that McDonalds, Coca-Cola and Adidas will pick up a tiny bit of the tab. ❐

©Natalie Haynes
41(2): 66/69
DOI: 10.1177/0306422012447748
www.indexoncensorship.org

Natalie Haynes is a comedian and writer. Her books include *The Ancient Guide to Modern Life* (Profile Books) and *The Great Escape* (Simon & Schuster)

INDEX
ON CENSORSHIP
Volume 37 Number 2 2008
MADE IN CHINA
中国制造
AI WEIWEI TRUTH TO POWER
ISAAC MAO FLIPPING THE SWITCH
YAN LIANKE DARKNESS VISIBLE
BRIAN GLANVILLE MEXICO 1968
REBECCA MACKINNON CYBER ZONE
PU ZHIQIANG PARTY RULES

MURDER IN MEXICO

Sports reporter **Brian Glanville** was expecting to cover the Olympics for the *Sunday Times* in 1968 – instead he found himself reporting the massacre of 300 students

The Olympic Games, like the poor, alas, are always with us. Drug ridden. Insanely expensive. Defying what the communists would call their own internal contradictions. Britain is saddled with them now, and God knows what they will cost in the end. But first, there will be China.

An awakening economic giant, caught between the Scylla and Charybdis of communist repression and rogue capitalism, perhaps the symbol and symptom of the Chinese Olympics is the poor wretches who fall to their deaths off the stadia they are building. Underpaid and underprotected. In Beijing, moreover, the pollution is such that numerous athletes will live outside the city. And Ethiopia's world-record marathon champion refuses to compete in China, fearing the pollution. We know that the Chinese government imposes ruthless censorship on the media and the Internet. Though fortunately, a grovelling attempt by the British Olympic authorities to prevent any kind of comment by their competing athletes has bitten the dust.

Abortive censorship was the name of the game, or the Games, in Mexico City in 1968. They were the third Olympics I had reported, for the *Sunday Times*, and I had decided they would be my last. I'd already written my novel *The Olympian*, which appeared in London and New York the following year. Essentially an allegory, using the figure of an English miler as a kind of Faust, driven to greater and greater illusory efforts. And I knew all too well the narcissistic self-involvement of the athlete, with his or her 'event'. Destined to be all too wretchedly exposed.

I arrived in Mexico City from Buenos Aires, where I'd been covering the torrid match between Estudiantes and Manchester United for the world club title. The

University students held at gunpoint in Tlatelolco, Mexico City, 20 October 1968
Credit: AP/Proceso

Olympics would begin the following week, but I had already been told to report on the so-called student riots. Only the previous day, the notorious blue-helmeted riot police, the Granaderos, had battered down the door of a barricaded polytechnic.

So, that first evening in Mexico, I was told to attend the student *mitin*, as it was called, in the Plaza de las Tres Culturas, at the end of the Paseo de la Reforma. Three cultures, comprising Aztec ruins, a Spanish colonial church and a vast, yellow-tiled apartment block, from one of whose terraces the student leaders would address the crowd.

It poured with rain, the students spoke; nothing happened. Speaking Spanish as I did, I found myself lurking round corners, talking to student activists. To be misled; they were convinced that nothing violent was going to happen.

So it was that when the bullets started flying in the Plaza de las Tres Culturas the following Wednesday night, it wasn't I but the amiable, modest *Guardian* athletics correspondent, John Rodda, who found himself lying prone on the student leaders' balcony, a secret policeman's gun jammed into his head, while bullets pinged off the wall behind him.

Earlier that day, we had travelled up together on one of the press buses from the Villa Olimpica, the Olympic Village, far from the centre and a kind of Shangri La for athletes. John told me he was going to the *mitin*. I told him that I wasn't, since I was certain that nothing exceptional would happen.

Early the following morning, I was phoned in my hotel by my *Sunday Times* colleague, John Lovesey, who told me that the previous night 'all hell had broken loose'. He had been roused from his bed to attend a press conference, to be told that there had been a riot in the square and a few deaths. Where the Mexican officials had seriously miscalculated was in their evident illusion that they were dealing only with a pack of dumb sports journalists. They may well have had a point when it came to the leathery old Americans, permanent adolescents, arrayed in their peaked caps and festooned with badges. When, a few days later, still shell shocked by the events, I ran into large, lumbering Arthur Daley, sports columnist then of the *New York Times*, and told him what had happened, his reply was, 'But that was just one section of the city.'

It would transpire that more than 300 students had been killed, their bodies taken to Campo Militar Numero Uno, to be burned. John and I visited the Plaza that Thursday morning. There was a huge scar left by a bazooka shell running down the yellow-tiled face of the apartments. Tanks stood in the square. Broken glass was everywhere.

The government, the Partido Revolucionario Institucional (PRI), which had been oppressively in power for 40 years, had seriously miscalculated. For sports journalists, notably those from England, Italy and Germany, turned into outraged investigators; to the fury of the PRI. And so we discovered *Por Que* and the brothers Mario and Roger Menendez Rodriguez. *Por Que* was a cheaply produced but defiant weekly magazine. John and I went to its offices, then on the Colonia Romana. There we found big, hefty, genial Mario and his handsome and more aesthetic brother, the younger Roger. They were scions of a well-known newspaper-owning family in Yucatan. *Por Que* that week was filled with alarming photographs of the atrocities committed in the Plaza by police and military. Indeed it was the soldiers who had surreptitiously ringed the square, and when a helicopter buzzed overhead and dropped flares, and the white-gloved secret police in the crowd had fired into the air, they had moved in, bayoneting and shooting.

Photographers knew they had no chance of having their pictures in their own newspapers. In a wily sort of censorship, the government of Diaz Ordaz controlled all newsprint, which would simply not be forthcoming for any newspapers which offended. So it was that the photographers took their pictures to *Por Que*.

Mario, its editor, told us that an attempt had recently been made to kill him. A coach had driven straight at him, but he had jumped in time onto the bonnet of a nearby Renault, so that the man standing innocently next to him had been murdered. John and I duly wrote our report for the paper, which was headed, with echoes of the ice-pick assassination of Leon Trotsky, 'Murder in Mexico'.

Meanwhile, at the Villa Olimpica, all was unawareness and indifference, as the athletes concentrated on their events. Sitting on the steep green bank above the training track, I tried to tell what had happened to the pretty, blonde Lillian Board, the English 800-metres contestant. 'I know it sounds terrible,' she rejoined, 'but I'm more interested in that girl down there. You see, I'm running against her.' A rare exception was the Northern Ireland pentathlon athlete, Mary Peters, who had heard that parents of the killed had been presented with their ashes.

John and I continued to work very hard on the appalling story, wondering the while whether we were under surveillance; even threat. We filed another comprehensive piece for the following Sunday, but to our frustration, it didn't appear. Those were the high, halcyon days of 'legendary' Harry Evans as editor.

A year later, I was back in Mexico City with the England football team, due to return in 1970 to contest the World Cup finals. It was to find Mario in solitary confinement, Roger and *Por Que* exiled across the Reforma to the grim Calle Xochimilko. Where Mario had kept his gun in his desk, Roger's lay on the top. He told me that lorry loads of the magazine had been hijacked.

Fast forward again to 1986. I am in Mexico City again, for another World Cup. Walking down a back street in the city centre, I see in a bookstall rack what seems a familiar publication. A magazine which closely resembles *Por Que*. The title is *Por Este* – 'for this' rather than 'why'. I bought it, opened it and there inside on the masthead are the names of Mario and Roger. With excitement, I telephone their office. Mario answers the phone. I tell him it's I. 'Oh yes,' he says casually, as though we'd seen each other the day before, rather than 18 years ago. I arrange to come over.

This I do with my friend and colleague Paul Gardner, an Englishman working for an American television company. There is a splendid reunion. Amazing stories to be told. How Mario was sprung from prison when a guerrilla leader had captured the Rector Elect of the University of Guerrero, and had exchanged him for political prisoners, Mario among them. How Mario had then taken off to spend years in Cuba, working on a PhD. How Roger, in the meantime, had been arrested and tortured, the printing presses of the magazine smashed up, Roger imprisoned. How a new, more democratic, president, Portillo, keen to improve relations with Cuba, had allowed Mario to return, Roger to get out of jail, the magazine paid compensation to restore its printing presses and to publish again: provided it changed its name to *Por Este*.

Since then, the long, corrupt monopoly of the PRI has come to an end. When the stifling autocracy of the communist regime in China comes to an end, who can guess? The colossal sums they have spent on their Olympics may or may not buy the propaganda success they so much want them to be. Since they no longer seem to be drugging their once all-conquering swimmers, gold medals in the pool will at least be, for them, at a premium. As for the Olympic Games themselves, they remain what they have so long been – a bloated, costly anachronism.

At least there is no longer the bitterly contentious figure of the Spanish reactionary Juan Antonio Samaranch presiding over the Olympic body. Nor yet that of the ineffable Avery Brundage, a Nazi sympathiser at the Berlin Olympic Games of 1936, still Olympic president in 1968 – the man who, when told that the celebrated Italian journalist Oriana Fallacci had been dragged by her hair down the steps from the students' balcony on La Noche Triste, replied: 'What was she doing there?' ❑

©Brian Glanville
41(2): 70/75
DOI: 10.1177/0306422012447745
www.indexoncensorship.org

Brian Glanville was the first ever sports columnist at the *Sunday Times*. His novel *The Rise of Gerry Logan* (Faber) was described by Franz Beckenbauer as 'the best football book ever written'. His non-fiction includes *The Story of the World Cup* (Faber) and *England Managers* (Headline)

LOCAL HEROES

Leah Borromeo meets East London residents who fear for the future of their homes and community in the wake of the Olympics

The motto of the Games is 'inspire a generation'. However, not everyone is enthused. Londoners from the poorest parts of the city face major upheavals, losing their homes, livelihoods and public spaces to a few weeks of medal-chasing over the summer. They believe that the Olympics gave local councils and big business an excuse for a land grab – in which the community has had little or no say. When they voice their opposition, they are hushed by the machinery of bureaucracy, the suppression of protest and the reality of losing the roofs over their heads. But their concerns are as real as the Games itself, which have received some £9.3bn in UK public funding. Community life will continue long after the athletes, the fans and the confetti have gone. I spent a week listening to and gathering the stories of Londoners shouting at the walls of an Olympic Jericho.

Joe Alexander, 38, is in property maintenance. He lives on the Carpenters Road Estate and is vice-chair of the local campaign group Carpenters Against Regeneration Plans.

I spent the day with Joe – a quiet, eloquent divorcee and father who moved to Stratford in London's East End in the hope of starting a new

The Carpenters Estate, in danger of being demolished as part of regeneration work being carried out near the Olympics site, East London
Credit: Leah Borromeo

life. We met at the Carpenters Arms, a green-trimmed pub at the edge of the Carpenters Estate – a housing estate of over 500 council units that may be demolished to make way for a new site for University College London after the Games. We cycled past its three high-rise tower blocks and through rows of single-family homes. It's quiet – a consequence of its residents being relocated to surrounding areas as far as the adjoining county of Essex.

Joe took me past many newly erected condominiums and demolished local businesses around its Greenway, a cycle and footpath, and down to an Olympic park viewing platform. It's a contrast of slick, brushed steel and half-buildings covered in debris and brick dust.

Night-time brings out an urban solitude. The three tower blocks are darkened and mostly empty – the result of the expulsion of most of their residents. 'The council moved people out giving all sorts of excuses like asbestos

... then rented out the top floors to the BBC,' a drinker at the Carpenters Arms explained.

The trauma of the wholesale uprooting of a community is evident at the pub. Once a bustling watering hole for local workers and residents, it now sits at the edge of a regeneration scheme that's more about the replacement of a close-knit working-class population in favour of a more isolated but economically richer 'gentrified' middle class.

Joe Alexander: I imagined regeneration would be a good thing and that the Olympics would help. I had this naive idea that these things assisted local communities. I also thought that residents would be involved in the whole process.

Regeneration plans were here before the Olympics. We're trying to ensure that we're not left behind. They gave Robin Wales, the mayor of Newham, an excuse to speed through plans he'd otherwise have more trouble with. The idea that the Games were a great thing was used to shut people up. People are worried about coming out against the Olympics because it looks like they don't want Newham or the country to benefit.

The mayor is in his third term and is going for a fourth. Everybody traditionally votes Labour, so he feels his office is safe and that he owns Newham. We feel he wants this legacy of creating a new Canary Wharf [so he can] say: 'I did that.'

Leah Borromeo: What sort of local support do you have?

Joe Alexander: We've had problems getting residents more involved. People are too busy trying to get by. So we've engaged with a few other campaign groups in Newham to share resources and collaborate.

We hosted a tour of the area that brought in a lot of people who didn't know what was going on. We took them around the estate and showed them a sustainable community that's been around for 40 years.

Leah Borromeo: What do residents want?

Joe Alexander: Stop this 'regeneration'. It may be too late and we may be aiming too high, but if we can't stop the regeneration we'd like to be part of the new one that's being created. I don't think that's a lot to ask for.

Council tenants are offered the chance to live in the redevelopments, but tenants aren't told they're losing their secure tenancies when they sign up. This could mean they could be forced out of their accommodation if they fall behind on their rent.

Because there's a benefits cap coming in, the local authority is restricting the number of local people living here. The council are making it harder for the poor to get housing within the borough.

The new Westfield Shopping Centre is meant to bring jobs to the area. But local agencies given the jobs of finding people haven't been hiring local people. We still have a huge number of unemployed.

We'd like to have the wider public know that there's a community in the shadow of the Olympic stadium and that we'd like to keep existing.

Although the Olympics have given us a platform for protest, we can't say we've benefitted. Every day we lose more of our homes. We live under the spectre of compulsory purchase orders. We don't have the luxury of time and are too busy trying to make ends meet and feed our families. So the legacy for us is that there is no legacy. These games are a tool used by the powers that be to get through the programmes they want to get us out – so they can move in a more economically worthy class. Once the Games go, we'll still be fighting this.

Julian Cheyne, 64, lives in Stepney – two miles from the Olympic park. He was one of many bought out by a compulsory purchase order (CPO) placed on the Clays Lane Estate – Britain's largest housing cooperative set up as an experiment to help vulnerable single people. The London Development Agency (LDA), the body which issued the CPO, said they had to clear the area to make way for the Olympic athletes' village. Despite his own disability – Julian suffers from myalgic encephalomyelitis, ME – he was part of a group of tenants that fought compulsory purchase and gained leave to hold a public inquiry into the decision. It was eventually dismissed in a High Court ruling and the 430 residents of the Clays Lane Estate were issued orders to leave by July 2007. The residents of ten bungalows and 50 flats were scattered across East London and were each given £8,500 in compensation.

Leah Borromeo: Tell me how you left Clays Lane.

Julian Cheyne: I was a long-standing resident. I had a lot to lose. I smelled a rat when Park Village, the university accommodation next door, was closed by the LDA. This housing had around 500 units like Clays Lane.

I contacted the LDA and asked why they were doing that. They said they were going to redevelop the area. I asked what needed redeveloping. They said it was something they planned before the Olympic bid. Why were they closing down a housing estate for students when it was

still perfectly functional? Then London won the bid and all those concerns were thrown out.

A mass eviction like this only works if you can downgrade the condition of an estate. LDA was making out that it was a derelict slum. But we had free parking, a community centre, a bus route into Stratford, and we lived next door to the Eastway Cycle Track which had woodland and a small stream. The Manor Gardens allotment was nearby, and in some parts of the walkway it's like you were in the country.

The LDA tried to spin it that this bit of green was disadvantaging us because we were being isolated – it was written off as being a 'scar' or an 'urban desert'. Complete rubbish.

The LDA came round and said Olympics or not, we had to move and showed us a plan [that wasn't dependent on the Olympics taking place]. I made a Freedom of Information request and found out there was no plan. In 2003, around the same time the bid went in for the Games, they raised the idea of us moving as part of a community and then sent a letter saying they'd consult with us about everything. They promised we'd get accommodation as good as, if not better than, what we had – which later changed to 'as good as but insofar as reasonably practicable'.

Leah Borromeo: What's it's like going through a compulsory purchase order?

Julian Cheyne: What you got was 'This is what is going to happen, like it or lump it,' LDA said nothing about the promises they made. It was 'You get what you get, you are being done a favour, stop being difficult.' I felt bullied.

We went through the whole process with them. Whether this was any good we don't know, because we still had to go. But we were arguing for the best deal we could get because this was a huge disruption to our lives. We still feel shortchanged. Because our community was so fragmented, we didn't work as well as we could have.

When the bid was won, I thought 'We're next.' And we were. When people talk about a housing legacy from the athletes' village, they never mention that they already knocked down housing for a thousand.

In the end, some of us stayed at the estate until the very last moment. I was there until five o'clock, when the estate closed on 23 July 2007, with another ten or 15 people.

Clays Lane has been erased, levelled. It's now going to be a back-of-house facility for the athletes' village. There's nothing there. Not even the name.

Leah Borromeo: What's the Olympic legacy?

Claire Weiss at Leyton Marsh, where the Olympic basketball facility is due to be built
Credit: Leah Borromeo

Julian Cheyne: Back in 2002, the government commissioned a report called Gameplan that said that the Games wouldn't improve sport participation – you're not going to improve people's health, don't expect increased tourism or economic benefits – this is just a national celebration. So the government already knew that but still decided to go for the Olympics.

It is quite baffling why London made the bid. At that time, the economy was bumping along nicely. You could argue this scenario: you take over a piece of land and set about a project to remake that in your city. You reshape the East End – along the lines of the Docklands model. You import the city, you import a new population and new culture. You economically colonise the East End. Colonisation in the guise of regeneration.

They couldn't have done this in West London because they'd come across too much opposition. But in the East you are dealing with poor people and an industrial history that's ripe for the picking if you're a property developer.

Here's a project that's sold as something that will benefit a poorer end of London but instead what you have is a transfer of assets, a transfer of land and a transfer of wealth. Regeneration doesn't mean the community stays while you improve its amenities. It means removing that community in favour of a more affluent group.

After the Games I think people will come away with the feeling they've been tricked. There is no legacy.

I met Caroline Day and Claire Weiss at the Leyton Marshes campsite occupation. Nearly two dozen tents, a field kitchen and a campfire greeted me on a misty weekend morning. This was Portisfield Meadow on Leyton Marsh – the site of the proposed Olympic basketball facility. The campsite straddled a large, fenced-off section of land next to long grasses, a tow-path, a canal and as much countryside as you could hope to see in London. Considering the London riots last year took place ten minutes down the road, this was positively rural. Behind the fence were diggers, enormous piles of rubble, guard dogs and what looked like the foundations of a building being laid. It all looked very sudden.

Caroline, 31, was the first to greet me. A local resident, she likes to run her greyhound around the Marsh. She's taken on the role of spokesperson for the Save Leyton Marshes campaign.

Claire is 64 and a former anti-apartheid campaigner. From a working-class East End Jewish family, she's lived in the area for over 40 years. Leyton Marsh has 'always been green' for as long as she's been there.

The day after we spoke, bailiffs visited the Save Leyton Marshes camp. They came with the police who arrested six protesters. Shortly after, the first Olympic anti-social behaviour order (Asbo) was issued.

Leah Borromeo: When did you find out about this building?

Claire Weiss: In December 2011, 250 letters were sent to the residents here about this. But if you're a resident of Leyton – which is a mile away – you got no consultation. Had we read some small print in a local newspaper that gets delivered before Christmas, we might have spotted it.

Caroline Day: That's deliberately minimal. No one would've seen it. It was a token gesture – in case we had a legal case they could say they had a screening opinion. There are local centres that could be used for basketball

– Hackney Community College and Barking Abbey School in Newham have one court each. Or they could have used one in Waltham Forest or Leyton or built on the site of the old Walthamstow dog track.

Claire Weiss: It's in the planning conditions that this building comes down and the land is restored after the Games. What we fear is that it's the thin end of the wedge – once this land has been used for this purpose, it stops being greenfield. If the authorities want to use it again, the planning permission for the use of the land has been granted and has set a precedent.

What we've found is that builders are going down half a metre under the soil to set in foundations. Under planning permission, it says that they're only going down a 'skim of 15 centimetres'.

Leah Borromeo: Do you know what we're breathing in from that pile of rubble?

Claire Weiss: Asbestos and lead. And an unexploded bomb. In the planning conditions, the allowance of earth is supposed to be covered so it doesn't spread contamination. As you can see, that's not covered.

Caroline Day: The soil contamination reports said that they couldn't identify any unexploded ordinance because there's such a high level of contamination in the soil. We can't even identify the bombs. That's what they've churned up on our marsh. Right next to an SSSI – a site of scientific special interest.

Leah Borromeo: What got you involved with this?

Claire Weiss: I found out about the Save Leyton Marshes group on Facebook. Went to the first meeting – the first idea was that we'd go through a legal route. I said 'We have to get down there and protest.' So every Saturday, we had a presence down here. The construction started in March. So we decided that we'd use the marsh in everyday ways and play some games. The first morning the lorries arrived, we stood in front of the lorries – myself and another person my age – and just chatted as people marked out a boules pitch. And we stopped the lorries.

Then one day the contractors just stopped work on the site. We think this coincided with the point they realised the geological problems they've come up against and we were a convenient smokescreen.

Leah Borromeo: Who is trying to stop you?

Claire Weiss: The Olympic Delivery Authority (ODA). They're the ones who want this built. They've leased this land for that very purpose. They don't want us to protest in the way that we have – or any other way either.

Leah Borromeo: What do you hope?

Claire Weiss: That we've blown a loud enough whistle and that this stops. Immediately. And they use local facilities. Then, that this site is restored to its original condition. We have to keep up the pressure that this happens. We don't want contaminated rubble tipped back into the land.

The ODA took us to the High Court for obstructing their vehicles. But the judge upheld that protesters had a right to protest. The Lee Valley Regional Park and the ODA waste public money by going through hugely expensive cases in the High Court over protest, and one of them tried to charge 'persons unknown' with £330,000 to compensate the contractors.

Leah Borromeo: If they don't stop this, then what?

Claire Weiss: We'll continue to protest, but there is no way we'll be involved in anything unlawful. There are many ways to protest. We won't break injunctions. The Save Leyton Marshes group isn't against the Olympics – we are against what is being done in the name of the Olympics. It's shameful. The spoilsports are these guys that destroy communities in the name of the Olympic Games.

Leah Borromeo: What do the Games mean to you?

Claire Weiss: A potentially positive force for people across the world to do something that is not warlike. What I don't like is that big business intervenes and that there are land grabs. Even the right to protest about that is being contested by the authorities. We don't want this. We want to keep the open space. In the middle of East London – a poor part of London – we need every green area we have.

Following the interview with Claire and Caroline, six protesters were arrested and police broke up the camp. Claire and Caroline sent the following response:

Four years ago this country rightly pointed out to China that it should allow peaceful dissent to take place and the voices of its people be heard during the Beijing Games. Yet here we have seen a peaceful protest by the local community and its supporters criminalised in order that an unnecessary, wasteful and even dangerous construction go ahead for the Olympics.

The authorities should have consulted, listened to and engaged with the local community. The local community has never been given answers as to why viable alternatives with legacy benefits were not chosen. The choice of this site has resulted in both a huge waste of resources and the use of force against people who only wish to protect their open green spaces. ❒

©Leah Borromeo
41(2): 76/87
DOI: 10.1177/0306422012448307
www.indexoncensorship.org

Leah Borromeo is a filmmaker and journalist

CAPITAL CLEAN-UP

Corinna Ferguson has concerns about the laws curbing protest ahead of the Olympics. The Games should not be a pretext for rolling out intrusive powers

On 27 July the Olympic Games, widely regarded as the world's greatest sporting event, will officially get under way in London after years of planning. Some 15,000 athletes and nine million spectators will descend on the capital for the Olympic and Paralympic Games, eagerly watched by a global TV audience of four billion. There's much national pride in being awarded the privilege of staging such a prestigious international event. But with the daunting opportunity come inevitable challenges, and there's also reason to be wary.

No one underestimates the task facing police and officials in delivering a safe experience for participants and audiences. But that cannot excuse infringements of basic civil rights such as peaceful protest and free speech. It would be completely against the original spirit of the Games for the occasion to become a sanction for loss of liberties and mass surveillance. This is London after all, not Beijing.

Sadly, we've already seen crackdowns on protest and free expression on the capital's streets. Westminster City council has introduced illiberal new bye-laws banning tents, sleeping gear and noise amplification equipment around Parliament, Westminster Abbey and Whitehall. These unjust restrictions are a disproportionate interference with the basic freedoms enshrined in our Human Rights Act. Unnecessary and over-broad, they were expressly designed to clear protesters from the streets ahead of the Olympics who 'spoil the visual aspect' and are likely to lead to undesirable confrontation between protesters and police.

The bye-laws empower police and designated council officers to stop a person from a 'prohibited activity' – using a tent or sleeping bag, for example – within the area. Failure to comply is a criminal offence, and the penalty could be £500. Items can also be seized, with police using 'reasonable force'. These offences clearly affect the rights of those wishing to protest by staying overnight – whether for a few days or, like the late Brian Haw, several years. The right to protest – including ahead of and during the Olympics – at Britain's heart of power is crucial to this country's proud history of peaceful dissent. Yet the council's reasons include the 'unsightly' nature of protest and the need to protect the area's 'amenity'. Yes – protest can be a nuisance, but isn't that often the point? The authority has failed to identify any actual harm that the bye-laws will prevent. Given the ample powers already available for dealing with truly damaging demonstrations, including the Public Order Act 1986, these new measures cannot be justified.

Then there's the London Olympic Games and Paralympic Games Act 2006. This legislation creates very specific powers, including regulations to curb advertising near Olympic venues and protect the event's commercial brand. But it's very broadly framed and allows a 'constable or enforcement officer' to 'enter land or premises' where they believe banned advertisements are on display and destroy material. Last time we checked, intrusive powers of entry were for fighting crime – not policing poster displays. The regulations do at least provide that advertising activity intended to 'demonstrate support for or opposition to the views or actions of

persons or bodies of persons, or to publicise a belief, cause or campaign or mark or commemorate an event' is exempt from the banning regime. But this sends a confusing message to police officers tasked with applying these powers in practice. The exemption must be robustly applied if peaceful dissent is to be respected.

Late last year, ministers also revealed that 13,000 military personnel will be stationed at the event, alongside G4S security guards. It's one thing putting troops on standby for genuine emergencies, quite another to militarise an international sporting event by flooding it with uniformed soldiers. The potential chilling effect on free speech is huge. Whitehall officials have also hinted at new powers for 'exclusion zones' in areas around Olympic sites, allowing for the fast-track forced removal of protesters. Following the disruption caused by a lone protester during the Oxford-Cambridge boat race, the Home Office ominously vowed to 'leave nothing to chance' to deliver an 'incident-free' Olympic Games.

But it's not only new powers that we need fear. The myriad of vaguely defined existing police powers is highly susceptible to abuse. Powers to stop and search without suspicion have been used disproportionately against ethnic minorities and peaceful protesters. While section 44 of the Terrorism Act 2000 was repealed following our successful challenge in the European Court of Human Rights, section 60 of the Criminal Justice and Public Order Act 1994 remains and suffers from the same dangerous flaws. It allows police to stop and search anyone – again without suspicion – in a designated area to see if they're in possession of weapons or potentially 'dangerous instruments'. The power to designate an area when it's 'expedient' to do so is incredibly broad and wide open to abuse and discriminatory application, hence the statistics showing that black people are 26 times more likely to be stopped under the power than white people.

While details of CCTV plans remain scarce, it's also been reported that a central police control room will be allowed to access any CCTV network in London and plot the information on a detailed 3D map. Given the sheer number of cameras in the capital, this could effectively enable targeted, real-time surveillance without any safeguards. The Metropolitan Police has also revealed plans to erect scores of new Automatic Number Plate Recognition (ANPR) cameras, focusing on Olympic venues. We're told that they're designed solely to increase safety and provide reassurance, but there's no effective regulation on how this sophisticated technology is used, who can be targeted, how long imagery is stored for and why.

The Games should be a showcase of all that's brilliant about Britain, a time to show pride in our history and traditions. They must not become a pretext for the roll out of intrusive powers in a misguided attempt to 'clean up' the capital. When the eyes of the world are truly upon us, what a shameful legacy for 2012 and our wonderful city that would be.

©Corinna Ferguson
41(2): 88/90
DOI: 10.1177/0306422012447764
www.indexoncensorship.org

Corinna Ferguson is legal officer for Liberty

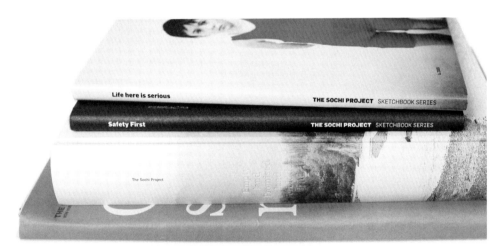

2
...WITH THE SUN ALREADY GLINTING ON THE POLISHED SHIELDS AND HELMETS OF LONDON'S COURAGEOUS RIOT POLICE, THE CEASELESS STACCATO CHIRRUPING OF THE SECURITY EQUIPMENT AT THIS GLOBAL SYMPHONY OF SPORT TUNING UP LIKE A WELCOMING DAWN CHORUS HERALDING IN ANOTHER DIURNAL ROUND OF STUPENDOUS SPORTING CONQUEST!!!

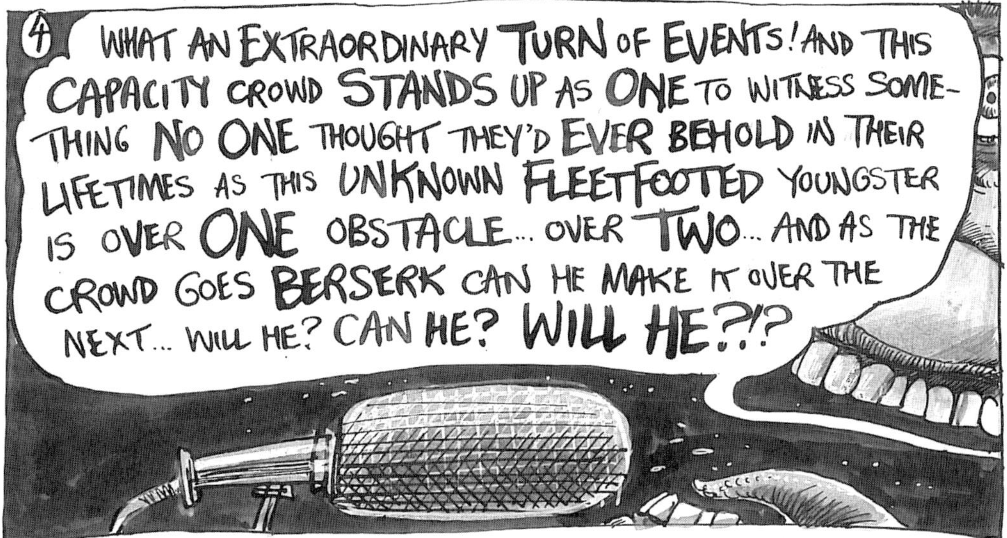
4
WHAT AN EXTRAORDINARY TURN OF EVENTS! AND THIS CAPACITY CROWD STANDS UP AS ONE TO WITNESS SOMETHING NO ONE THOUGHT THEY'D EVER BEHOLD IN THEIR LIFETIMES AS THIS UNKNOWN FLEETFOOTED YOUNGSTER IS OVER ONE OBSTACLE... OVER TWO... AND AS THE CROWD GOES BERSERK CAN HE MAKE IT OVER THE NEXT... WILL HE? CAN HE? WILL HE?!?

6
...TO BE HONEST IT SERVES THE TERRORIST BASTARD RIGHT FOR TRYING TO SMUGGLE IN A BURGER 'N' FIZZY DRINK NOT PRODUCED BY ONE OF THE GAMES' MANY GENEROUS CORPORATE PARTNERS! BUT NOW LETS GO OVER TO THE OLYMPIC DUNGEONS FOR THE 2nd HEATS IN THE SYNCHRONISED ANAL PROBE! GARY?
HI GARY! AND... OOH! THAT MUST SMART!
YAAWN!!

PUTIN'S WINTER CHALLENGE

The 2014 Winter Olympics border a troubled region.
Arnold van Bruggen reports. Photos by **Rob Hornstra**

We first visited Abkhazia at the end of 2007. During the Soviet era it was one of the richest regions, a province of Georgia. It attracted millions of tourists. But a bloody civil war in the early 1990s left it in ruins. Some 200,000 Abkhazian live as refugees in Georgia and beyond. The country is empty, which is perhaps one of its most striking features. We returned with a fairy-tale story about this Soviet relic, accompanied by photographs of hotels overgrown with moss, and full of the dreams of the people who live there and those who were driven out in the 90s and hope one day to return. A forgotten paradise on the Black Sea that hardly anyone had heard of.

A month later Vladimir Putin visited Guatemala, where the International Olympic Committee was gathering for an important meeting. In a rousing speech in fluent French and English, Putin made a final bid to bring the Winter Olympics to Russia. 'Sochi is a unique place,' he said. 'On the sea-shore you can enjoy a fine spring day, but up in the mountains it's winter.' His pitch worked: Winter Olympics on the border of the empty country we had just visited, and on the other side of the mountains from violent republics such as Dagestan and Chechnya. This was our reason for starting *The Sochi Project*, a five-year-long documentary project about the region surrounding Sochi.

Sochi lies on the eastern shore of the Black Sea. From the coast, the narrow strip of land rises quickly to meet the steep peaks of the Caucasus. The mountains act as a natural buffer against the cold of Russia that stretches endlessly behind them. Sochi has a sub-tropical climate. Its pebble beaches are bordered by tea plantations, tangerine and palm trees. The coastline is dominated by large hotels and sanatoriums that overflow during the long summers with tourists from across Russia – few foreigners come here. On the long boulevards, the noise of Russian chansons mixes with the smell of sweat, *shashlik* and sun cream. Sochi is Russia's summer capital. Despite the proximity of Abkhazia and the North Caucasus, this area has been untouched by war and violence. Ask any Russian whether Sochi is in the Caucasus and he will deny it. Sochi is a different entity. It represents that first holiday romance and summer fun. The Caucasus represents bombings, violence, backwardness perhaps, folklore and good food. The Caucasus stands for the wild, hairy men you wouldn't want to meet in a dark alley in Moscow.

Perhaps it does not matter whether Sochi is in the Caucasus or not. But it is likely that Sochi will soon have to face facts. An attack on Putin's prestige project would be the crowning glory for the separatists from the North Caucasus. FSB chief Alexander Bortnikov expressed concerns back in 2010 about the security situation surrounding the Games. Earlier bombings in the

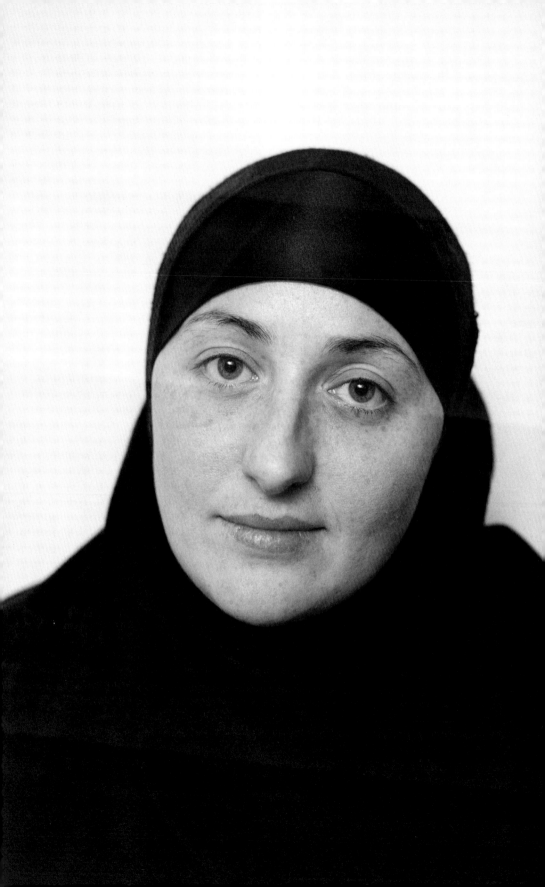

Moscow subway and airport, and the hostage crises in Beslan and Dubrovka Theatre, were evidence that the terrorists could operate with apparent ease far from home. How easy would it be for them to attack an Olympic target on their doorstep?

It was clear that this region would change dramatically between 2007 and 2014. Sochi would be transformed from a resort town to a winter capital – no mean feat in itself. But observers were also curious to see how Moscow would address the instability in its backyard. What to do about Abkhazia and the North Caucasus?

The first problem was solved surprisingly quickly. In early August 2008, war broke out between Georgia and Russia. Tensions that had simmered for years over Georgia and its breakaway provinces Abkhazia and South Ossetia, and between the Kremlin and Saakashvili's government in Georgia, escalated into a five-day war. At the end of August, President Medvedev recognised both provinces as countries. It was an unexpected move. Russia had always been opposed to recognising Kosovo because it was itself faced with Chechnya, Dagestan and Ingushetia. And now it was recognising Georgia's Kosovos? However, the decision brought calm to this part of the Caucasus. The United Nations was expelled from Abkhazia and the region came under Russian military control. Sochi no longer bordered a conflict zone, but – in Russia's eyes at least – a recognised country. Russian border troops now guard not only the Russian border directly adjacent to the Olympics, but also the Abkhazian border with Georgia 200 kilometres to the south.

The Russian government is still working on a solution to the second problem. Billions of roubles from the Kremlin are propping up the regimes in the North Caucasus, the aim being to remove support for the Islamic-inspired terrorist and separatist movements by providing employment and economic development. Alexander Khloponin has been appointed Special Envoy to the North Caucasus. In recent years he has launched fantastic initiatives, including the construction of five ski resorts in the region. The separatists responded by killing a busload of Russian tourists near the slopes of Elbrus, Europe's highest mountain, and sabotaging ski lifts. A prolonged battle between separatists and security forces in the snow on the border with Dagestan and Chechnya last February was proclaimed on a rebel website as training for Sochi 2014.

The average unemployment rate in the North Caucasus is 50 per cent. Moscow finances up to 91 per cent of the budgets of the North Caucasian republics. In Kabardino-Balkaria, Ingushetia and Dagestan, violence has increased to such an extent it almost qualifies as civil war. During our visits to the areas, it also seemed to us as if support for the separatists is increasing rather than decreasing. The desperate situation there is not the only cause. Nowhere in Russia are human rights as violated as in the North Caucasus. Human rights organisations such as Memorial have their hands full defending young men wrongly convicted of having terrorist links. The European Court of Human Rights is almost swamped by cases brought against the Russian government by families whose sons or fathers have been kidnapped by security forces. In Moscow, we visited safe houses where Chechen women, fearing death at the hands of their husbands or brothers if family honour was at stake, hide before fleeing to Western Europe. Russia appears so far to have been unable to improve the situation. In Dagestan, a rape case is currently being heard in which the alleged perpetrators were given legal assistance by the police. When the president of Dagestan himself became involved in the case, it seemed justice had run its course. At the eleventh hour, the defendants' lawyers succeeded in getting the girl to drop the rape charge. 'If you pay a lot of money to the police and prosecutor you can have a charge dropped,' a young woman in Dagestan told us. Her husband is serving a 14-year prison sentence. She does not have the money. 'In our villages young men are faced with a diabolical choice. You are either threatened by the police, or you are threatened by the separatists.'

All of Russia's problems come together in the North Caucasus: corruption, a lack of democracy and gross human rights violations. It is perhaps particularly cynical then that this is the region in which the Winter Olympics are intended to present Russia's new face to the world. ❏

Captions

All photos © Rob Hornstra/INSTITUTE
Page [2]: Former ballroom in Pitsunda, Abkhazia
Page [4]: Khava Gaisanova, whose husband was kidnapped by unknown men in the North Ossetian capital Vladikavkaz. Because there were no eyewitnesses to the crime, no trial took place
Page [5]: Khava Gaisanova and her family, including her husband
Page [6]: After separatists threatened Isita Isaeva, aged 28, and her husband, they went to the police. But the police accused her husband of a series of murders and only allowed prison visits after he confessed to the crimes. He has now been in prison for 14 years

©Arnold van Bruggen
41(2): 94/100
DOI: 10.1177/0306422012448151
www.indexoncensorship.org

Find out more on thesochiproject.org. You can also follow The Sochi Project on Facebook and Twitter @thesochiproject. Support the project and receive the next annual publication about the North Caucasus

THROWING SPARKS

ABDO KHAL

Banned in Saudi Arabia, Kuwait and Jordan

Out in the UK in September 2012

Winner of the 2010 International Prize for Arabic Fiction (IPAF)

The author is a former fundamentalist preacher, now a hard-hitting and controversial novelist

'Abdo Khal shines a light on life at the bottom of the heap, in Saudi's often forgotten villages. His voice blends image-rich poetic classicism with contemporary patois, which makes for an unmistakably Arab mix,' - *The Guardian*, UK

REQUEST A COPY

If you are interested in receiving an advance copy of this controversial novel, particularly if you write for a blog, paper or magazine and would like to review it, please contact me directly at **Sophia.Blackwell@Bloomsbury.com**

TEAM LUKASHENKO

Belarus's dictator is an ice-hockey fanatic. Should the rest of the world boycott the 2014 games? **Natalka Babina** considers a propaganda coup

The window of my apartment in Minsk looks out onto a huge structure in the form of a grotesque-looking hockey puck. It is known as the Minsk Arena, a sports complex built specially for international ice-hockey tournaments, and it stands as a symbol of the sporting ambitions of the Belarusian authorities. In addition, the Minsk Arena acts as the regime's visiting card, because the government and sports administrators are hoping that, in 2014, the world ice-hockey championships will take place right here, on this skating rink, in a stadium designed for 15,000 spectators.

Hockey is the favourite sporting activity of the Belarusian president Alexander Lukashenko. Every year he organises hockey tournaments in which he himself participates and wins. A Belarusian oligarch – on whose companies the EU recently imposed economic sanctions – has admitted in an interview that he goes to play hockey with Lukashenko much as he goes to work. If you play hockey with the president and join him in the gardens of his residence, mowing the grass with a scythe, you are in with the Belarusian elite. So 'welcome to Belarus', all you visiting competitors!

President Alexander Lukashenko during an ice-hockey match, Minsk, September 2003
Credit: Alexander Polyakov/RIA Novosti

In Belarus there are many so-called Ice Palaces – vast edifices with ice-rinks designed specifically for hockey tournaments and built at Lukashenko's personal instruction. On the whole they are empty. When matches do take place, schoolchildren and students are forcibly hustled in to play the part of spectators. Before a match everyone is carefully checked and frisked. Why? Well, how would it look if anyone displayed a political banner or the forbidden national white, red and white flag in public, which has become a symbol of national resistance? On one occasion my 10-year-old nephew was instructed to remove a white scarf with a red strip down the middle before going into the Minsk Arena. When his father expressed outrage and threatened to surrender their tickets, he was allowed through, but a security official sat with the boy throughout the match in case he thought to brandish the seditious scarf.

As I write, Siarhei Kavalenka is starving in a prison psychiatric ward, solely because he raised the national flag on New Year's Eve in his home town.

Does Siarhei Kavalenka need the championships in Minsk – assuming he survives?

Do my nephew and his father need them?

Does the Belarusian oligarch?

But there can be no doubt at all that those who do need the championships in Minsk are none other than Lukashenko and his team.

What do international sporting organisations have in mind as they plan the championships in Minsk? Is it all about popularising ice-hockey? Organising a festival for hockey fans in Belarus? Earning a bit of money? Enriching the Lukashenko clan?

If it's the last of these, then success is certain. All the Ice Palaces, along with most hotels and restaurants in Minsk, belong to the Presidential Administrative Directorate – for which read Lukashenko. So the money is sure to end up in the right pocket.

Any other possible agendas the sporting organisations may have in view remain hazy.

As regards popularising hockey and organising festivities for Belarusian fans, I must confess I'm not particularly interested in professional sport and all I know about ice-hockey is that you have to get the puck into the other team's goal. In my view, funding allocated to any sporting championships, wherever they may be held, would be better spent feeding the hungry or treating sick children. Please don't bother to read on if you disagree. But if championships like this do take place, the beneficiaries of the events should be the people of the country in which they are being held. At the present time Belarus is in no condition to hold festivals of any kind.

The people of Belarus are living in a state of persistent hardship and oppression imposed by the regime in power. As the Russian poet Mandelstam once wrote: 'We live without feeling the country beneath our feet.'

We have felt this hardship particularly over the past 18 months. The blatant fraud associated with the presidential elections; the cruel, bloody suppression of peaceful protests; the false evidence given during the trials of the protesters; disastrous financial collapse; a mysterious explosion in the metro for which many people have blamed the authorities themselves; and the summary punishment of people who may or may not have been terrorists – irrespective of the fact that over 150,000 people signed a petition against the death penalty.

Immorality, demonstrative cruelty, an intentional flouting of law human and divine, chronic lying, national discrimination – all these characterise the actions of the authorities on a daily basis.

Threats, beatings, house searches and provocation dominate the lives of civil rights activists and the independent media in Belarus.

Sudden impoverishment, lack of civil rights, and deep despair that comes from knowing that it is impossible to change things are experienced daily by ordinary people.

I shan't presume to say anything about the daily life of oligarchs – I know nothing about it.

I've tried putting the following question to a number of people: 'How do you view plans to hold the ice-hockey championships in Minsk?' Typical responses included remarks such as:

'Unimpressed. In my mind hockey is associated with Lukashenko and he's not a figure who makes me feel comfortable. So neither does the prospect of the championships.'

'It would be fine, but not now.'

'Not at all. I worry about surviving on my pension, and helping my children who live in poverty on a miserable salary. Hockey leaves me cold.'

I recall a recent conversation that took place when I was queuing in a bank, in the small town where I live. As they waited their turn, people chatted about how unprecedented devaluation had left them three times poorer overnight; about the rising prices of subsistence goods, what to do, and how to live.

'According to the constitution, in this country power lies with the people. We need to change the government,' I said.

A protester holds the banned opposition flag during celebrations to mark
the 15th anniversary of Belarus's independence, Minsk, 25 August 2006
Credit: Vasily Fedosenko/Reuters

Everyone burst out laughing.

'When you get hit on the head with a truncheon, it hurts – a lot…' said a middle-aged woman after a hearty giggle.

So there you have it: an average conversation. People do not feel that power lies in their hands, nor do they have the leverage to change their lives. And in terms of what the authorities offer, people see only the truncheons wielded by the special forces.

So let's distract them with a bit of hockey! It's just what everyone needs!

The decision rests with international sports organisations. If they decide to hold the world ice-hockey championships in Minsk, they will be offering the authorities the perfect gift, as well as a propaganda coup. For the Belarusian people, for civil society, it will be yet another insult. It will confirm the imperative that the authorities are diligently imposing on Belarusian society: 'Morality is nothing: it is a hollow invention. The globe turns on money and coercion. The central values in the world are possession and power. That is the system we are building here in Belarus. The whole world lives like this. The world supports us, so don't even think of trying to resist.'

I hope that those who take the decisions in world hockey support the basic values we share as human beings: do not kill, do not lie, do not commit adultery, respect your own people. The authorities in Belarus do not share these values and are doing their best to ensure that Belarusians also forget about morality and human dignity. If the thought of shaking hands with representatives of this regime does not seem rebarbative, then by all means hold the championships in Minsk. Only remember that the hands you shake sign documents that impose prison sentences on people who are trying to defend their constitutional rights. Belarus is ruled by ochlocracy – the power of the worst.

Belarus and the Belarusian people are treading a path that may be familiar to many other nations, a path that leads, as the classic Belarusian poet Yanka Kupala wrote, to a state that lets us 'call ourselves human' and 'not be as cattle'. It is a path that will allow us to define our own lives, freedom and dignity. Let there be no doubt: Belarus shall achieve this. But help from the outside is also important. Holding the ice-hockey championships in Minsk will act as a powerful shot to the advantage of Lukashenko and his team of hockey-lovers, and send the puck over the goal-line of Belarusian society.

Any dictator knows the value of both pop music and sport. In a political dictatorship song and sport cease to be any kind of refreshment (which is what they should be) and become, essentially, instruments of propaganda. In Belarus every sport has its curators amongst government officials. Their ready declarations on how sport should be dissociated from politics are pure demagogy. Sport *is* a factor in politics. If it contributes to the support of an unethical order, then it becomes a factor in a particularly repellent kind of politics. And even if sport should indeed be dissociated from politics, should it be dissociated from ethics as well?

It should not, or disaster is bound to ensue.

I may appear to exaggerate, but that is reality as I see it. There is a limit to immorality beyond which nemesis awaits. The authorities have taken us to this limit. I can't say what kind of disaster threatens: a loss of independence; an accident at the nuclear power plant currently under construction in Belarus; some awful terrorist attack at the world championships, similar to that in the Minsk metro a year ago?

If all this does not take us as far as terrorism, it will certainly lead to acts reflecting the despair of Belarusians who have not yet lost their 'inner moral perception' or forgotten how to look at the stars. The International Federation must be prepared.

In Belarus it is a criminal offence to call for sanctions against the ruling regime. This means that I could be arrested for writing this article. However, I shall not be calling for the championships to be moved elsewhere, not because I'm afraid of prison (which I am) but simply because I don't feel competent to offer advice to specialists.

Instead, let me simply present a few facts.

Over the past 17 years, all elections in the country have been rigged. This is something Lukashenko himself has seen fit to recognise.

The country has always held political prisoners, who are used by the authorities as leverage to achieve their own ends. At present there are 13 political prisoners in the country. Two candidates for the presidency were arrested on the day elections took place in 2010 and released 16 months later in April.

Peaceful protests are crudely and violently suppressed.

Lukashenko admires Hitler and the system he enforced in Germany.

The country is effectively lawless, legal decisions are taken by the imposition of 'telephone law'.

In his public addresses, Lukashenko likes to describe European politicians in the following way: 'they haven't got the balls ...'; 'goats'; 'scumbags'; 'a lousy bunch'.

According to sociologists the majority of the Belarusian population does not object to the idea of transferring the championships from Minsk to a different country.

If, under the circumstances, the International Ice Hockey Federation feels that it is either moral or logical to hold the championships here – then by all means let them do so. ❏

Translated by Irena Maryniak

©Natalka Babina
41(2): 102/108
DOI: 10.1177/0306422012447754
www.indexoncensorship.org

Natalka Babina is a writer

The Telegraph
Ways With Words
Festival of Words and Ideas

Dartington Hall
Devon
6 – 15 July 2012

Ten days of books, ideas and inspiration
in the heart of the South Devon countryside.

Join world-class authors and speakers this summer as we celebrate the 21st Ways With Words festival; one of the UK's most loved literary events.

Set in the stunning medieval courtyard and gardens of Dartington Hall.

Full programme available in early May.

Call **01803 86 73 73**
or check online at
www.wayswithwords.co.uk

2012 programme to include:

Michael Palin
Hilary Mantel
Claire Tomalin
Jeremy Vine
Joanne Harris
Andrew Miller
Mark Easton
Simon Jenkins
Michael Buerk
Roy Hattersley
Michael Frayn

. . . and many more.

CHINA'S PROMISE

China pledged to improve human rights when it hosted
the Olympics. **Duncan Hewitt** considers the legacy

On a hot July night in 2001, the streets of Beijing erupted with jubilation, as crowds celebrated the International Olympic Committee's (IOC) decision to award the 2008 Games to the Chinese capital. Amid the euphoria, there were warning voices too – that the planned reconstruction of parts of the city would lead to more demolition of Beijing's unique architectural heritage, and that the desire to achieve the perfect Games would only strengthen the government's controlling impulses. The Chinese authorities, who had learned their lesson from a failed bid to stage the Games eight years previously, told the world loudly that not only would they give the world an Olympics to remember – but also pledged that the Games would make China more open, and leave a legacy of improved human rights.

Seven years later, few denied that the authorities had delivered on at least one of their promises. A global TV audience saw a spectacular Olympics, with the world's best athletes competing in stunning venues, designed by some of the world's top architects, on which no expense had been spared. Other events took place against spectacular scenery, including the Great Wall outside Beijing. The opening ceremony, choreographed by famous film director Zhang Yimou, took viewers' breath away, as did the firework 'footprints' across the Beijing sky, designed by the celebrated artist Cai Guoqiang.

The Chinese capital's creaking infrastructure experienced a dramatic upgrade, from the opening of Norman Foster's third terminal at Beijing Airport, to the much needed expansion of the city's public transport network, with new subway lines and high speed rail links to other Chinese cities. Beijing's notoriously poor air quality was given a boost too, as the enormous Shougang steel works was largely closed down and moved outside the city limits. The temporary closure of construction sites and many other factories, along with restrictions on the number of cars on the streets each day, also contributed to unusually clear skies – though this particular benefit was to prove short-lived.

In terms of human rights, the legacy was always going to be more complex, and progress arguably more difficult to achieve. In a sense, the Olympics fed into a process of change which was already well under way in China, involving significant movement towards greater openness in society. At the same time, the government and party, determined to maintain their absolute power, sought to consolidate their control, in part out of fear at the long-term implications of this continuing opening. The jailing of human rights activist Hu Jia in April 2008, for example, was seen as a clear warning sign to other dissidents not to cause trouble or embarrassment for the government in the Olympic year.

If the police tried to block access, they had to give us a good reason

Still, the Games exposed China to the glare of international scrutiny to a greater degree than the country had ever experienced. Whether or not the authorities were serious when they made their pledges back in 2001, they now had little choice but to at least offer the appearance of taking action, as the world sought to hold them to account. One example was the brief round of talks between China and representatives of the Dalai Lama shortly before the Games, following riots in Lhasa and other Tibetan regions. These were the first talks for many years (and there have been no more since).

One pledge which the Chinese government made in its application to stage the Games was that it would offer journalists full and unfettered access to the whole country in the run-up to the Olympics. This aroused much cynicism from journalists used to China's traditionally tight controls on foreign reporters, who had always been required to have special accreditation from the government, and, in theory at least, to apply for permission from local authorities before visiting any part of China other than the city where they were based.

In fact, this was one area where the Chinese authorities appeared to deliver. From the beginning of 2007, foreign reporters – with the proviso that they were accredited by the government to work in China – were told that they would be allowed to go anywhere in the country (with the continuing exception of Tibet) without needing specific permission, and would be allowed to interview anyone who was willing to talk to them. It was, on one level, a significant breakthrough: 'It meant that the rules were on our side,' as one veteran Beijing-based foreign correspondent puts it. 'No longer could local police simply kick us out of their areas just for being there – if they tried to block access, they had to give us a good reason, whereas in the past we were the ones who had to justify why we were in a particular area without prior permission.'

In practice, however, the authorities, perhaps inevitably, responded by becoming more creative in finding other ways to limit what journalists could see. Individuals connected to sensitive topics which the government did not want the foreign media to report – such as critics of forced relocations and human rights activists – found themselves being 'reminded' by the authorities that perhaps they did not want to be interviewed by foreign journalists. In the immediate run-up to the Games, a number of the most prominent dissidents and activists were taken away from their homes for periods of several weeks, while there were also farcical scenes when reporters tried to visit the home of one dissident in Beijing shortly before the Games began, and were greeted by a police cordon around the entire area which the authorities said was due to roadworks.

Tension between China and the international media was also heightened following rioting in the Tibetan capital Lhasa in March 2008, when the Chinese authorities accused a number of major media outlets of bias, saying they had depicted a violent anti-Chinese riot by Tibetans as a crackdown on peaceful protesters by Chinese troops. Foreign journalists who had travelled to Lhasa were ordered to leave. And subsequent international criticism of China, and disruption of the Olympic torch relay by pro-Tibet protesters, was portrayed by Beijing as just another part of a global anti-China conspiracy,

A sign declaring Tibet's support for the Beijing Olympic Games greets foreign reporters as they enter Lhasa, 27 April 2008
Credit: David Gray/Reuters

and led to the founding of a website, anti-cnn.com, which channelled public anger towards foreign journalists – some of whom received death threats.

Nevertheless, to the surprise of some observers, the relaxation of the rules on foreign correspondents' movements in China continued after the Olympics – though this was not part of the government's original pledge – and remains in place today. The authorities also took a very different approach following the riots in Urumqi, capital of the mainly Muslim north-western region of Xinjiang, the following year: they set up a press centre in the city the next day and invited foreign reporters to visit.

Still, there has since been much surveillance of journalists who visit the region – and several cases of people being arrested or jailed after speaking to foreign journalists. Reporters covering sensitive stories may still face harassment and even violence. These problems reached a peak following online calls for protests in Chinese cities inspired by the Jasmine uprisings in the Middle East and North Africa in early 2011. Several foreign journalists were beaten, simply for being at the scene of the proposed protest. Many more were detained, then subsequently called in again by the authorities and filmed while being questioned, a rare occurrence in China. Some were also threatened with expulsion from the country if they continued to report the story. Journalists who complained that, under the new rules, they were allowed to report on anything they wanted were told by Foreign Ministry spokeswoman Jiang Yu that they 'should not seek to use the law as a shield'.

Other specific human rights pledges also proved problematic for the authorities. Although they promised that they would establish official 'protest zones' in three parks around Beijing – conveniently located far from the Olympic stadium and central area – almost none of the many protesters who applied to stage demonstrations received permission. 'Freelance' protesters who sought to unveil pro-Tibet slogans, meanwhile, were bundled away by the authorities, who also harassed foreign media trying to cover the scenes – and in several cases subsequently deported some of them from the country.

The Games were also accompanied by a 'clean-up' of Beijing, which not only led to many migrant workers losing their livelihoods in the city and being effectively forced out of town for the duration of the Olympics, but also to the jailing of several activists, including people whose homes were demolished to make way for Olympic facilities or infrastructure projects. There does seem to be evidence that the Games contributed to a growing role for China's internal security services in influencing policy at a high level. Beijing's desire for the Games to be perceived as a success around the world meant that the authorities left nothing to chance. A massive security cordon was thrown around the city – and also around other cities only peripherally involved in the Games (like Shanghai, which hosted a few soccer matches). Military police were posted at underground stations, and passengers were forced to go through security checks before boarding trains. Many bars and entertainment venues were also ordered to close for the duration of the Games. Along with tight controls on access to the Olympic Green and other areas where sporting events were taking place, it led some to dub the event the 'no fun' Olympics. Certainly the party atmosphere so notable in Sydney in 2000 was conspicuous by its absence, with tight visa restrictions on foreign visitors for the whole of 2008.

The strategy was echoed during the Shanghai World Expo two years later, when what was ostensibly a fun, family-oriented event was run more like a military operation. There were training exercises featuring police frogmen repelling armed attacks on the Expo site from the neighbouring Huangpu River, and a huge police presence both at the site, where military

A Uighur woman demands the return of members of her community to Urumqi, Xinjiang, during a visit by foreign journalists to the region
Credit: Ng Han Guan/AP

police could often be seen marching through the crowds, and throughout the city: two military policemen stood at attention outside every entrance to every underground in the city for the entire six months. The subsequent jailing of dissident intellectual Liu Xiaobo, along with the tough line on human rights lawyers, and harsh treatment of artist and activist Ai Weiwei also hinted at this growing security role in Chinese society. In 2012 China declared that it was hoping to 'export' its security methods for use at other global events in the future, such as the 2014 football World Cup in Brazil.

Yet, despite this, society did continue to open. As well as loosening restrictions on the foreign media before the Games, Beijing briefly also allowed greater access online to information from abroad, unblocking the BBC's website for the first time in almost a decade, for example (though it later re-blocked the Chinese language section of the website). The authorities were under pressure to offer unlimited internet access to journalists and others attending the Games, and there's no question that the Chinese internet became more open that year. Indeed, according to the Chinese internet expert Isaac Mao, this opening up of the web had a significant long-term impact: by giving people a glimpse of what they were missing, he believes it contributed to growing public demands for greater web freedom, and greater openness from government and in society in general. Certainly the voices of ordinary Chinese people have grown louder over the past couple of years, aided by the spread of microblogs – and the authorities are at least paying far greater lip service to responding to public opinion.

Some pundits have also suggested that the Games encouraged public debate about China's international image: there was much criticism online when it was discovered that a little girl who apparently sang beautifully at the opening ceremony was in fact only lip-synching to a recording sung by another child, whom officials had deemed not sufficiently photogenic to be allowed on stage. There was also a controversy over the pre-recording of some of the sequences of firework 'footprints' in the sky over Beijing at the ceremony. Public anger at such fakery was compounded shortly after the Games, following revelations about a huge scandal involving baby milk formula adulterated with melamine, which had killed several children and harmed thousands of others. The fact that this news had been covered up for many weeks, partly due to government rules banning the Chinese media from reporting 'bad news' about food safety scandals during the Games, added to public anger at officials placing image above the health of ordinary citizens.

Despite all the controversies, the Games were arguably a landmark on China's path towards a greater engagement with the outside world. As promised, the Olympics brought 'China to the world, and the world to China'. For ordinary Chinese people, it was a first chance to see many of the world's top sporting stars and, with a few exceptions, world leaders, gathered in their country – even if for most this was only on TV. This not only gave them the sense that their country was more connected to the outside world, it also made many people feel that China was being taken seriously – something significant in a country with a festering sense of historical humiliation by foreign powers in the 19th and 20th centuries.

As a result, the Games, which were regarded by the authorities as a great success, also contributed to a growing confidence – on the part of China's government and many ordinary people – about the nation's standing in the world. This sense was quickly reinforced by the global financial crisis later the same year, when China became a much sought-after investor, widely looked to as a guarantor of international financial stability.

Yet while such confidence may help remove bitterness and anger about the past, some fear that it might, on the other hand, lead to more of the type of belligerent nationalism shown by some of the 'anti-CNN' protesters. And the Beijing Olympics themselves may similarly be seen, in retrospect, as a double-edged sword. On the one hand, they seem to have encouraged the government's controlling impulses, helped the establishment hone its security procedures, and gave the government something of a propaganda boost. But they also arguably contributed to moves towards a growing openness and demands for greater freedoms – even if this is not quite what the Chinese authorities originally intended when they spoke of the Games bringing progress in human rights to China. ❐

©Duncan Hewitt
41(2): 110/118
DOI: 10.1177/0306422012447913
www.indexoncensorship.org

Duncan Hewitt is a former BBC China correspondent who now writes for *Newsweek* and other publications from Shanghai. He is the author of *Getting Rich First - Life in a Changing China (Vintage)*

SPRING THAW

The media in Burma is greeting the retreat from censorship with suspicion. Sports journalist and former political prisoner **Zaw Thet Htway** reports

An eminent satirist whose send-ups have antagonised the Burmese authorities for the past 20 years is fuming under the Rangoon sun. His piece mocking the mismanagement of the Ministry of Communications, Posts and Telegraphs has been banned. 'The notion of Burmese media's Arab spring is total bollocks. The dawn of freedom of the press, huh? Our writings are still in the grip of the Dark Ages!'

He is not joking. As freedom of the press is still under threat, the recent thaw on media censorship in Burma has had a mixed response. Despite rumours that the Press Scrutiny and Registration Division will cease to exist when a law on printing and television is passed by parliament in June, local editors continue to complain about the restrictions they face on a daily basis.

Last June, information minister Kyaw Hsan announced the removal of censorship for publications in five areas: arts, technology, health, sports and children's literature. Economy and law were added to the list in December, followed by education this month.

News and religion are the only two areas that still have to go through the press scrutiny board. Out of 212 weekly journals and 189 monthly magazines

Zaw Thet Htway after he was released from prison, 13 January 2012, Rangoon
Credit: Khin Maung Win/AP/PA

published in the country today, 73 journals and 65 magazines still have to have their contents screened and approved by the board.

In February, a reporter from *Modern Journal* was sued by the authorities in Thapeikkyin Township in Mandalay Division for publishing an article about the condition of dilapidated roads in the area. In March, the Ministry of Mines threatened the *Voice* with a lawsuit after the weekly disclosed that several government ministries, including the Ministry of Mines, did not come clean in the auditor general's annual report. Such intolerance of the press undermines the government's rhetoric about building a modern democratic nation and casts doubt on their commitment to reform.

Minister Kyaw Hsan, formerly a brigadier-general, may be no different from his predecessors in telling journalists how to do their job. In his words, we should 'follow journalistic ethics such as impartiality, describing a subject from various angles, not from one single angle, in order that the people can review and decide correctly, exercising freedom and accountability and freedom and rationality, ensuring unity in democracy and upholding the national cause in exercising unity in democracy'.

Setting down rules is never going to be popular with the media. Senior journalists who were trained in Burma's post-war parliamentary era shrug off these rules, saying that a media law is not really necessary for professional columnists.

Since President Thein Sein highlighted civil society's role in democratic transition and encouraged the formation of civic groups in his annual speech in March, many government-organised NGOs have been rolled back. The Myanmar Film Association was the first to become independent with a new organisational structure voted in by film professionals. Other pro-government associations are likely to follow suit.

When the Myanmar Writers and Journalists Association was dissolved on 24 March at an emergency meeting of the Ministry of Information, three new associations were created, for writers, journalists and publishers. The formation of fully independent media associations has not, however, been encouraged – the information minister has made it clear that he would like to see an umbrella organisation for all media groups, a Press Council modelled after similar councils in neighbouring countries.

In response, poets, journalists and writers who would rather stand on their own identities and principles have unionised. Myanmar Poets Union chaired by Maung Seine Ni, Myanmar Journalists Union, chaired by Daw Aye Aye Win of Associated Press, and Myanmar Writers Union, chaired by Htat Myat, have been formed as bottom-up initiatives.

Whatever the future holds, the unions are committed to the lifeline of the fourth estate: freedom of the press. They will certainly be watching over the development of top-down media associations and the government's media law. ❒

Translated by Ko Ko Thett

© Zaw Thet Htway
41(2): 119/121
DOI: 10.1177/0306422012447765
www.indexoncensorship.org

Zaw Thet Htway is a sports journalist. He was sentenced to 15 years in prison in 2008 on multiple charges including 'inciting offences against the state'. The sentence was later increased to 19 years. He was released in January in a mass amnesty of political prisoners

CCTV camera near the Olympic Stadium, London, 28 March 2012
Credit: Sang Tan/AP/PA

SPY GAMES

Katitza Rodriguez and **Rebecca Bowe** warn of threats to privacy as surveillance plans get underway for the Olympics

Surveillance and security around the Olympics is intensifying from country to country, purportedly to prevent terrorism and serious crime, and activists are increasingly concerned about a growing trend: once the Games are finished, authorities rarely cut back on public surveillance. With the pricey new infrastructure installed for good, individuals' rights to personal privacy are at risk of being permanently diminished.

London already bears distinction among privacy watchdogs as being one of the most closely surveilled cities in the world, yet routine security practices pale in comparison with the exhaustive measures to be imposed during the 2012 Summer Olympics. Surveillance and security measures were recently described in the UK's *Independent* newspaper as the 'biggest operation since the Second World War' to be undertaken by UK intelligence agency MI5 at a cost approaching 1bn. Plans call for the installation of a new monitoring and intelligence gathering system, plus the mobilisation of nearly all of MI5's 3,800 agents. While details of the intelligence-gathering programme remain classified, it appears to be intended for long-term use.

As London beefs up its security infrastructure, Brazil has already begun mapping out a security strategy in anticipation of the 2016 Olympics in Rio de Janeiro. The situation there is shaping up to be another cause for concern, particularly because the government seems eager to follow London's lead. According to Agence France Presse (AFP) reporter Javier Tovar, Brazilian security agencies plan to use surveillance drones, tough border controls and IP-based surveillance systems.

Brazil will also host the World Cup in 2014, run by the international governing body for football, Fifa. For both competitions, most of the events will take place in poor suburbs of Brazilian cities, where the homicide rate is among the highest in South America. According to market analyst firm 6Wresearch, a spike in Brazil's video surveillance market can be attributed to both a rise in crime and the anticipation of hosting two major international sporting events. The surveillance measures are largely going unchallenged – there seems to be little public debate or attention focused on these issues or the privacy implications they present.

Brazil's video surveillance market generated US$124.96m in 2011 and is expected to reach $362.69m by 2016, the largest share in the overall market. Research analysts predict a compounded annual growth rate of nearly 24 per cent from 2011 to 2016. 6Wresearch expects 'a shift towards more secured IP-based surveillance systems' since advantages include 'low cost, video analytics, remote accessibility and [are] easy to integrate with wireless networks'.

A security blimp flies over the Acropolis, Athens, 9 August 2004
Credit: Andy Clark/Reuters

No sooner had Rio been selected in 2009 for the Games than the US government sought to strike a partnership with the Brazilian government on security and information-sharing strategies, according to secret diplomatic cables released by WikiLeaks. In December 2009, the US embassy in Brazil sent a cable to the US government entitled, 'The future is now'. The message encouraged the US to use the Olympic Games to justify the expansion of its influence over Brazil's critical infrastructure development and cyber security measures. By highlighting concerns about the possibility of power outages or breakdowns in infrastructure, particularly in the months leading up to the Games, the US government could justify a bid for increased co-operation with Brazil on counterterrorism activities. There were 'opportunities for engagement on infrastructure development' and 'possibly cyber security', the cable stated. In a second cable, sent on 24 December 2009, the embassy again emphasised its interest in broadening US objectives in Brazil. 'Taking advantage of the Games to work security issues should be a priority, as should co-operation on cybercrime and broader information security,' it read.

In the lengthy diplomatic exchanges between the US embassy in Brazil and the US government, the absence of any reference to the very serious privacy, civil liberties and public accountability implications of widespread surveillance technologies stood out as a glaring omission. The same could be said for current public discourse in Brazil. So far, there has not been any significant criticism of the security and surveillance measures being introduced – in marked contrast to the UK, where privacy campaigners have been active.

Brazil's safeguards for privacy in the face of such pressure aren't especially promising. An impact assessment is needed to evaluate whether cameras installed to help combat crime in Rio are necessary and to ensure that these measures do not become an Olympic Games legacy, especially if there are less intrusive methods of combating serious crimes. There is no legislation pertaining to the privacy of personal information in Brazil, but a draft bill that, if introduced, would protect the collection, use and disclosure of this information is under consideration. It remains to be seen whether the bill will bypass privacy protections by allowing exemptions – namely, databases created for the sole purposes of public security, national security or law enforcement activities.

It's too early to say exactly what security and privacy protocols Brazil will keep once the 2016 Summer Olympic Games end. But if history is any guide, there is reason to believe that a surveillance regime ushered in by the Olympics will continue to pose threats to individual privacy well into the future. Privacy advocates, having assessed the range of measures implemented in connection with previous Olympic Games, warn of a 'climate of fear and surveillance' that could have a detrimental effect on 'democracy, transparency, and international and national human rights law'.

The proliferation of surveillance technology around the Olympics is hardly new. Greece's contract with technology company Science Applications International Cooperation (SAIC) called for the creation and support of a C4I (command, control, communications, computers and intelligence) system to 'allow Greek authorities to collect, analyse, and disseminate information' by leveraging SAIC's expertise in telecommunications, wireless communications and video surveillance. The technology blends data-mining data-matching and profiling capabilities. Those researching this area have referred to the adoption of such security measures as an emergence of a 'super-panopticon' and a 'marriage of camera, computers and databases'.

One report revealed that Greek law enforcement and intelligence agencies installed more than 1,000 surveillance cameras in Athens in advance of the 2004 Summer Olympics – and then continued to make use of them for policing purposes long after athletes and spectators had packed up and left. While the stated purpose for the continued use of the cameras in Greece was to monitor traffic, the report found that they were actually employed to monitor public spaces – including during political demonstrations. This revelation triggered heated exchanges between law enforcement officials and the Greek Data Protection Authority, leading to the resignation of the authority's head, Dimitris Gourgourakis, and his deputies. At the time, Gourgourakis stated that police use of surveillance cameras 'directly breached' privacy regulations. In 2007, the country's data protection law was amended to exempt surveillance cameras from its privacy provisions.

The use of surveillance cameras in Athens barely registers in comparison with the all-out monitoring campaign Chinese authorities implemented in 2008, when the Olympic Games were held in Beijing. Chinese authorities installed 200,000 cameras and employed other surveillance measures in an effort to make Beijing secure. And, in a move that drew widespread condemnation, the government ordered foreign-owned hotels to install internet monitoring equipment to spy on hotel guests.

When it was announced that Vancouver had won the bid for the 2010 Winter Olympic Games, Canadian civil society organisations feared a repeat of the security measures adopted by Greece and China. Privacy advocates called for the government to remain open and transparent about the necessary security and surveillance practices that were planned; they demanded a full, independent public assessment of these measures after the Games and sought to prevent 'a permanent legacy of increased video surveillance' and other security measures. 'It is already clear that the event allowed for new surveillance technologies to gain a foothold in Vancouver that would never otherwise have been accepted,' noted Tamir Israel of the Canadian Internet Policy and Public Interest Clinic.

The message appeared to get through. In the run-up to the Games, the Office of the Privacy Commissioner of Canada, in conjunction with the Office of the Information and Privacy Commissioner of British Columbia, issued recommendations to prevent security measures from unduly infringing individual rights. 'The duty of governments to provide for the security of citizens must, in democratic societies, be tempered by the values that underpin our way of life,' said Jennifer Stoddart, Privacy Commissioner of Canada. 'The right to privacy must be upheld, even during mega-events like the Olympic

Games, where the threat to security is higher than usual.' At this critical juncture, the agencies seeking to implement security measures in London and Rio would do well to heed her words.

Violations of individuals' privacy can range from the loss of anonymity in public places to the inability to communicate and associate freely with others. The capabilities of Closed Circuit Television (CCTV) have risen dramatically, and due to the relatively low cost of the technology, street cameras are now everywhere. Technological advances make it possible for CCTV to perform surveillance tasks similar to electronic wiretapping and intelligence sharing; identification systems can link images not stored on databases with images that have actually been archived. Given the prevalence of this technology and how easy it's become to identify one unnamed face amidst thousands, people who care about anonymity may have a very difficult time protecting their identity in the imminent future.

While it's important to take security precautions prior to the Olympics, these actions should not result in the implementation of public surveillance without regard for personal privacy. It's crucial that the public scrutinise the security and privacy measures the Brazilian government is considering. There must be an informed and open debate about privacy and security.

Most importantly, the public has a right to know whether enhanced security measures will be removed after the Games. The true spirit of the Olympics as an opportunity for cultural exchange ought to be preserved. Using the Games as an excuse for curtailing civil liberties violates this spirit. ❏

© Katitza Rodriguez and Rebecca Bowe
41(2): 122/127
DOI: 10.1177/0306422012448767
www.indexoncensorship.org

Katitza Rodriguez is international rights director at the Electronic Frontier Foundation (EFF).
Rebecca Bowe is international privacy coordinator at EFF

Ivan Klíma
The girl athlete

*A popular novelist and short story writer in the
sixties, the Czech writer Ivan Klíma has not
been able to publish any of his work in Prague
since the cultural freeze that followed the
Soviet invasion of 1968. This story (' Koulařka '
in Czech original) appeared last year in the
second issue of* Spektrum, *the unofficial
magazine put out in typescript by banned
Czech authors and printed in London by*
Index on Censorship.

Vicky owed her successful career chiefly to
Olda Rudinger, the well-known world record-
holder in the discus (83.20m Dublin 1988).
He had played his part, first and foremost,
by making his good, quiet wife Mary pregnant,
and then of course also by insisting that she
take the recently discovered (and soon to be
prohibited though still surreptitiously used)
Anabol praenat. At the time dosage had not
been properly tested and poor Mary had
either been exceptionally susceptible to the
drug, or she had simply taken excessive doses.
Before she had even reached the sixth month
of her pregnancy, her doctor anticipated that
the foetus would be far larger than normal,
and he lost no time in sending Mary to
hospital.

The child, a female, was born two months
premature. It weighed a full thirteen and a
quarter kilograms and measured 72 centimetres. It came into the world with the aid of
a Caesarian operation. Its muscles (and in
particular the biceps) were so astonishingly
well developed as to be monstrous; its head,
on the other hand, was tiny by comparison.
Indeed, its skull may even have suffered some
slight deformation during the difficult birth,
but this did not impair the child's basic
physiological functions, nor its movements.
The mother, however, failed to come out of
the anaesthetic and died three days later. The
cause of death was given as 688 (' Other, non-

specific, post-natal complications '), which
was not exactly accurate in view of the
above data.

The father decided to christen his daughter
Victoria, no doubt having her future career
in mind when he picked the name.

Until she was six, little Vicky was looked
after by Olda's mother, the old Mrs Rudinger.
Her health and nutrition were from the
beginning under the supervision of an elderly
doctor from the Central Sports Institute (CSI).
The child developed much as expected. At
four years of age it started to jabber, at five it
stopped wetting itself, at six attained a weight
of a hundred kilograms, and at seven
managed, for the first time, to reach 20 metres
in the shot put with a six-kilogram ball. It
was then that her father decided that Vicky,
who had hitherto only trained sporadically,
must be removed from the none-too-suitable
environment of his mother's home and placed
in the year-round care of the CSI boarding
school. He himself became her coach.

Vicky accepted this change in her circumstances without demur. She was of a somewh
phlegmatic disposition, showing little interest
in such matters. Even though she was now
quite capable of forming short, simple
sentences or shouting, in unison with the
other pupils, such exhortations as ' Come on
Faster! Hip, hip, hurrah! Give 'em hell! ',
she spent most of her time in complete silen
sucking the thumb of her right hand, and
speaking of her own volition only at meal
times whenever she wanted a second helpin,
On such occasions it was even possible to
detect traces of emotion in her demeanour.
' Please, dear cook, may I have fifteen mor
dumplings? ' Once, having added a particu
larly large piece of meat to the girl's plate,
the elderly cook noticed that there were te
in Vicky's eyes. ' What's the matter, child?
she enquired. ' I love you! ' whispered Vi

THE GIRL ATHLETE

Czech writer **Ivan Klíma** was banned after the Soviet invasion of 1968. This satire first appeared in the samizdat *Spektrum*, published by *Index on Censorship*

Vicky owed her successful career chiefly to Olda Rudinger, the well-known world record holder in the discus (83.20 metres, Dublin 1988). He had played his part, first and foremost, by making his good, quiet wife Mary pregnant, and then of course also by insisting that she take the recently discovered (and soon to be prohibited, though still surreptitiously used) Anabol praenat. At the time dosage had not been properly tested, and poor Mary had either been exceptionally susceptible to the drug or she had simply taken excessive doses. Before she had even reached the sixth month of her pregnancy, her doctor anticipated that the foetus would be far larger than normal, and he lost no time in sending Mary to hospital.

The child, a female, was born two months premature. It weighed a full 13-1/4 kilograms and measured 72 centimetres. It came into the world with the aid of a Caesarian operation. Its muscles (and in particular the biceps) were so astonishingly well developed as to be monstrous; its head, on the other hand, was tiny by comparison. Indeed, its skull may even have suffered some slight deformation during the difficult birth, but this did not impair the child's basic physiological functions, nor its movements. The mother, however, failed to come out of the anaesthetic and died three days later. The cause of death was given as 688 ('Other, nonspecific, post-natal complications'), which was not exactly accurate in view of the above data.

The father decided to christen his daughter Victoria, no doubt having her future career in mind when he picked the name. Until she was six, little Vicky was looked after by Olda's mother, the old Mrs Rudinger. Her health and nutrition were from the beginning under the supervision of an elderly doctor from the Central Sports

Institute (CSI). The child developed much as expected. At four years of age it started to jabber, at five it stopped wetting itself, at six it attained a weight of a hundred kilograms, and at seven managed, for the first time, to reach 20 metres in the shot-put with a six-kilogram ball. It was then that her father decided that Vicky, who had hitherto only trained sporadically, must be removed from the none-too-suitable environment of his mother's home and placed in the year-round care of the CSI boarding school. He himself became her coach.

Vicky accepted this change in her circumstances without demur. She was of a somewhat phlegmatic disposition, showing little interest in such matters. Even though she was now quite capable of forming short, simple sentences or shouting, in unison with the other pupils, such exhortations as 'Come on! Faster! Hip, hip, hurrah! Give 'em hell!', she spent most of her time in complete silence, sucking the thumb of her right hand, and speaking of her own volition only at meal times whenever she wanted a second helping. On such occasions it was even possible to detect traces of emotion in her demeanour. 'Please, dear cook, may I have fifteen more dumplings?' Once, having added a particularly large piece of meat to the girl's plate, the elderly cook noticed that there were tears in Vicky's eyes. 'What's the matter, child?' she enquired. 'I love you!' whispered Vicky, using the phrase for the first and only time in her life.

When she was nine she consumed two kilograms of meat a day, plus the same quantity of bread and fruit, 15 eggs, three one-litre bowls of boiled rice or potatoes, and 38 assorted pills; she drank five litres of milk and only slightly less fruit juice. She weighed 185 kilos and, with her six-kilo ball, threw 28 metres every time. She ran 30 kilometres a day, did 400 bends and 600 push-ups, while lifting a 50-kilo dumb-bell a hundred times was mere child's play to her. She could also handle some less difficult mathematical exercises (such as three plus two or four minus one), on occasion showing herself capable of more complicated sums (two times two or even four times three). As, however, any abstract mental effort tended to exhaust her, the doctor recommended that in future she be given a restricted curriculum, and so her knowledge of mathematics progressed no further. In her spare time she liked to turn the pages of picture books, and where the illustrations were accompanied by brief captions of no more than one sentence she managed to read them, when not too tired.

A simple operation, carried out shortly after her 11th birthday, ensured that she would not, every month, have her fitness undesirably impaired. And three months later she made her international debut. Her splendid throw of 29.60 metres gave her second place behind the phenomenal Kulagina (30.15 metres), making her one of the great hopes of our athletics. Kulagina, together with the slightly younger Hammerschlag, were her only serious rivals. She never did manage to beat Kulagina, despite the intensified training schedule which helped her overcome the 30 metre barrier by the time she was 13.

Fate was kind to her, however, for Kulagina was to collapse and die in training shortly after setting an astonishing new world record of 33.89 metres (sudden arrest of heart function), while Hammerschlag, having for some time suffered from cartilage trouble in her right elbow, gave up the shot-put and continued her sporting career as a long-distance runner.

Thereafter, Vicky had no rivals to touch her. At 15 she mounted the Olympic rostrum to take her first gold medal, and a year later bettered the world record of the deceased champion. From then on she could only improve on her own records, throwing an unbelievable 40 metres within four years of her Olympic triumph.

By this time she had, of course, grown to womanhood. She stood 207 centimetres tall and weighed 302 kilograms. When she strode towards the shot-put circle, her gait measured and seemingly lumbering, the spectators usually fell silent as if in amazement, even awe, and at such times her footfalls appeared to be causing the earth to thunder. The petrified hush lasted while her gigantic body, with its comic, as if superfluous, tiny head, froze in complete concentration, while it made its heavy-footed half-turn before finally unleashing the terrible lever with the miniscule fingers at its end. And the hush continued as the heavy iron sphere sailed through the air as though it were a ping-pong ball; suddenly it gave way to a loud, mostly unarticulated roar, which grew mightier and mightier, before turning into a triumphant chant. Now she could, from time to time, make out the constantly repeated two syllables: Vi–cky, Vi–cky! Above the heads of the crowd there rose a forest of arms, of clenched fists, raised in homage to her. At moments such as these she became aware of a feeling of intense pleasure deep down in her bowels; spasms in her vagina gave her a sensation of bliss, soft groans issued from her lips, and her own arms flew up in the air. It looked like a gesture denoting joy, or perhaps a greeting for the assembled fans, but in fact it was completely involuntary, a movement not governed by her will. The sensation of utter bliss exhilarated and exhausted her at one and the same time. She was able to bear it once more when she took her second throw, sometimes even the third, but after that all strength seemed to be drained from her body. That was why, as everyone knew, she excelled in the first three throws and never improved on the results achieved in them. As often as not, certain of her victory, she would give up after the third, provided of course her coach and father permitted her to do so.

It happened on occasion that she did not throw as well as she wished or as the crowd expected. Then, the silence would continue, interrupted only now and again by an isolated cry of dismay.

When this happened, she felt something that could be likened to the sorrow of a jilted lover. Slowly she would put on her gigantic tracksuit, make her way to the dressing-room and weep. She sobbed when her coach and father came in, when

SPEKTRUM

The third issue of SPEKTRUM is to be published in February 1981.

SPEKTRUM is an unofficial Czech magazine produced under difficult conditions by writers whose work cannot appear in the official media.

SPEKTRUM 3 concentrates on historical topics — Jan Hus, Czechoslovak independence in 1918, T G Masaryk, 1968 — and the poetry of Karel Siktanc.

Other authors are Zdeněk Kalista, Milan Uhde, Jiří Němec, Milan Kundera, Josef Vohryzek, Stanislav Mareš, Zdeněk Neubauer and Jan Lopatka.

274 pp ISBN 0 904286 27 4
Price £5 or US$12

SPEKTRUM 1 and 2 are still available:

Spektrum 1 (pub Aug 68) had the world and its problems as its theme and included the poetry of Bohuslav Reynek. 150 pages.
ISBN 0 904286 06 1   £5/$12

Spektrum 2 (pub July 79) carried articles on philosophical and theological subjects and the poetry of Emil Juliš.   192 pages.
ISBN 0 904286 09 6   £5/$12

For further details write to:
Index on Censorship
21 Russell St, Covent Garden,
London WC2B 5HP
Telephone 01-836 0024

the reporters crowded round, she just went on crying as if she would never stop, and no one could get a word out of her. When, however, the competition went well, she would lavish sentences, even whole clauses, on everyone within range, having laboriously been taught them beforehand by her father and coach or by the secretary for moral welfare; and once she had uttered them, they became the property of the nation, being heard on radio and TV more frequently than the words of the most prominent poets, not to mention philosophers. ('If it weren't for all these marvellous people backing me, I'd never have achieved my record!' 'You know, I really thought I wouldn't make it, but then I said to myself I had to, the people expected it of me.' 'Sport is, first of all, a hard slog, and that's why I respect everyone who puts in a good day's work.')

She now had a fairly good comprehension of the world in which she competed. She knew that one had to stretch to the limit in order to come first. But, of course, not everybody *could* get to the top, only the best made it. Those who won the most often were the very best – they were successful – and deserved the highest acclaim. She also knew that there were people who never came first, and others who didn't even try. Even such individuals, no matter how useless their existence might seem to her, had to be treated politely.

She was given only very occasional glimpses of the non-athletic world, spending all her time between the sports field, her bedroom, and the institute canteen. When she did chance to stray beyond the bounds of the sports centre and found herself in streets full of strangely dressed people wearing all kinds of clothes unsuited to any event, where some nonsensically wasted their time queueing for potatoes, meat or cauliflower while others crammed into overcrowded trams, people would turn their heads to look at her and not infrequently called out to her. This worried her so much that she was afraid it might adversely affect her form, and she hurried back to the institute. She could not wait to get back in her track suit and jersey and make up for lost time.

She travelled a great deal and thus saw many different stadiums and, out of the windows of coaches and cars, many foreign streets, inscriptions in incomprehensible languages, and foreign crowds. All this she barely took in, dozing or eating on the coach so that, as soon as they arrived, she would be able to jump out and resume her training.

When she was 20 (she now weighed 316 kilos, the biceps of her right arm measured 97 centimetres, her chest 273 centimetres, and her world record stood at 40.60 metres) she suffered a severe blow. Crossing the athletic field, Olda Rudinger was struck by a flying hammer, which fractured his skull, and he died on the way to hospital.

His daughter and protégé inherited a large collection of medals, discuses, cups, plaques, the training schedule for the following quarter, a batch of jerseys which had belonged to the greatest discus throwers, a collection of track shoes once owned by the greatest triple jumpers, the manuscript of his unfinished book, *My Life with the Discus,* and a three-room flat in a high-rise building in the centre of the sports complex.

She went to his funeral and wept as she was used to weeping in the corner of the dressing room when things went wrong. She was sorry she would never again hear her coach and father encouraging her, egging her on: Go to it, Vicky! You can do it! Vicky, you must! It's now or never, Vicky! She wasn't at all sure whether she would still be able to go to it, to do it, without that encouraging voice of her coach and father to spur her on.

The funeral took longer than expected and Vicky was two hours late for lunch. She ate 37 rissoles (seven more than usual, and she wasn't sure whether this was out of sorrow or just that she was so famished), put on her jersey and track suit and went off to train.

On her 27th lap she realised that something was missing. No one was waiting for her with a towel and a jug of lukewarm fruit juice, no one called out: 'Stick it out, Vicky!' She felt a chill run down her spine and tears started to her eyes.

Vicky Rudinger loped off the track and like a runaway racehorse ran across the grass until her huge foot plunged into some cavity and was trapped in it while the rest of her body, propelled by its massive momentum, continued on its course.

A bone could be heard cracking and Vicky's bulk crashed to the ground.

They took her to hospital with a fractured femur, laid her in a specially reinforced bed, put her leg in plaster and raised it in a sling, telling her she had to remain absolutely still. That same afternoon her fellow athletes came to visit her and wish her a speedy recovery. When they left she lay there waiting for yet another visitor. And it was not till the evening that she realised she was waiting in vain, that her coach and father would never come again, and she wept once more. For supper she could only manage eight schnitzels (they had, of course, taken her to the special CST hospital) and wondered whom they would appoint as her new coach and whether she would not get out of condition after this enforced break in training.

They released her two months later. Her new coach was waiting at the hospital entrance with her training schedule. And she again ran, did callisthenics and push-ups, lifted dumb-bells and put the shot as she had done before, but when, after half a year's arduous training, she only once succeeded in exceeding 35 metres (the 15-year-old Kotovova had by this time brought off several 40-metre throws), it was clear to everyone that Vicky Rudinger was in all probability finished as a top athlete.

They tried sending her to several less important meetings where she finished second or even third, but when after the contest she sat weeping in the dressing-room, no one came to ask how come she had not done better.

They now knew she would never do better. She had several visits in her new apartment (she had left everything just as it was while her coach and father was still alive, only putting her own cups, diplomas and medals in one of the glass cases) from officials of the Athletics Association, who did their best to find out whether there were any complications in her life. She certainly did not know of any. Then they suggested that she might like to take on some coaching work. At first she declined, but after several months of inactivity she was ready to agree. They invited her to take part in a seminar, at which she was to comment on methods of training. She did not comment, and they realised that this was beyond her. After that she received no more invitations, nor did they send her to the next training camp. She still kept making her appearance at the stadium, accompanied by her coach, who gave her unnecessary advice and tried in vain to step up her training schedule; she was still given her special rations in the canteen, enough to feed ten hungry navvies; and she went on living in the sports centre where no one turned to stare after her and no one shouted at her that she was too big and too strong. Yet she felt that something was not right, that she was beginning to be different from the others – she was not performing and thus was no longer useful.

Before going to bed, having finished her last evening stint of bends and push-ups and taken her last refreshment of the day (15 eggs and half a loaf of bread), she sat in the armchair she had inherited from her coach and father (it had a lever on either side which could be used to press down strong steel springs in order to build muscles) and, her eyes shut, dreamt of the time when she would at last find her form, return to the shot-put circle, make her throw, and the crowd would emit its triumphant roar which would fill her with bliss.

When she was tested for the next competition she threw a mere 31 metres, and that was definitely the end. They said they could no longer afford to feed her for nothing. They rambled on about starving mankind (as if it was her fault) and that the people would not forgive them such wanton waste. They offered her several civilian jobs, all of which she turned down for she was not used to work, nor did she have time for it. She had to carry on training hard if she wished to regain her form.

Then they took away her coach and told her she had to move out of the sports centre, forbidding her entry to the CSI canteen. But since she was, after all, a former world record-holder (the 16-year-old Kotovova, that new 360-kilo superstar of world athletics, had just thrown 43.20 metres), they let her have a nice two-room attic flat on a housing estate and gave instructions that she be elected chairwoman of the local branch of the Union of Women Fighters for Lasting Peace. This post brought with it a special food ration for heavy manual workers.

And so, at 20 years of age, Vicky for the first time entered a world in which no one competed on track and field, in which instead of putting on jersey and track suit in the

Soviet athletes parade in the opening ceremony of the Olympic Games, 26 August 1972
Credit: Mondadori Portfolio/Getty Images

morning and going out on to the track, people hurried to board overcrowded buses which took them to their places of work; a world in which instead of 15 eggs you had two slices of toast with jam (or often without) for breakfast. She gazed numbly at the queue outside the food store, and when they put four rolls, a quarter of a loaf of bread, a quarter of salami, a jar of jam and a tin of liver paste in her basket, saying that this was her ration for the day (true, she was also entitled to sugar, rice, and flour or potatoes, but none of these was in stock today), she went red and tears came to her eyes. 'But what shall I eat?' she asked the shop assistant. 'The same as you did before', replied the girl, giving her a dirty look. 'You couldn't get as fat as this on normal rations.'

She wanted to tell them all she was Vicky Rudinger, the same Vicky they used to cheer and applaud, but she could not speak. Her massive triple chin trembled and she picked up her feather-light shopping basket and left the shop.

That afternoon, attending her first meeting of the Union of Women Fighters for Lasting Peace, she was incapable of bringing her mind to bear on anything but the terrible realisation that, having eaten the four rolls, quarter loaf of bread, quarter of salami, liver paste and jam in the morning, she would now have to spend the rest of the day and the whole night suffering the pangs of an unendurable, gnawing hunger. Fortunately, the meeting was chaired by the vice-chairwoman. She spoke about the continuing food crisis in a world now inhabited by eight thousand million people. Vicky could not imagine what a thousand million people was, and so she found herself unable to concentrate. How could she get back in condition when they let her starve like this? How could they do this to her, hadn't she always trained conscientiously? Why had they lost confidence in her?

Returning home from the meeting she saw that right behind the high-rise block of flats there was a small wood with a nice expanse of grassland which she could use for training – if … She was shaking with hunger. Her teeth chattered uncontrollably. She went inside the wood and chewed some blades of grass and a piece of bark she peeled off an oak-tree. Running three laps round the wood, she returned home. There she sat in the armchair she had inherited from her coach and father and stared at the glass case full of cups and medals. Somewhere in the vicinity she could hear a TV going, someone was stomping about in the flat above. An iron ball lay in the middle of the display inside the glass case, the one she had used when she beat her own last world record. Summoning up all her strength, she picked the ball up and went out to train.

Grasping the ball in her hand, Vicky made her half-turn and threw it in the direction of the wood. Then she measured the distance. Twenty-six, at most 27 metres. She recovered the ball, returned home, put it back in its case, sat down and cried. In the course of the next month she lost 99 kilos in weight. Her legs shook so badly that she could hardly stagger to the shop to claim her meagre food allocation. Waiting in the potato queue she fell in a dead faint. They did not even call an ambulance, just poured some water over her, and there was hatred in their voices as they talked about 'people who stuff themselves with food'. Why couldn't they understand that she was starving, starving to death?

Her journeys to meetings of the Union of Women Fighters for Lasting Peace became more and more exhausting, until in the end she was forced to suggest that they hold them in her apartment. No one raised any objections, some of the members were quite curious to find out what her flat was like. The treasurer, a buxom, always-hungry pensioner who had been manageress of a meat shop and could not now, in retirement, get used to the frugal ration for non-workers even though her successor slipped her an extra piece of gristle every week, cherished a secret hope that Vicky would provide them with refreshments. (The cow *had* to be getting privileged treatment, how else would she have got so fat? Though the treasurer had to admit that she did seem to be losing a little weight just lately.) They

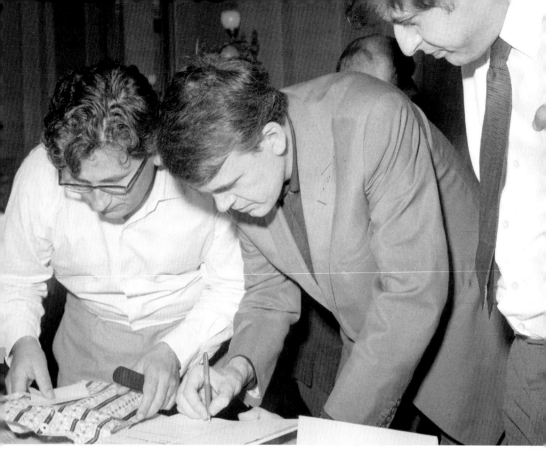

Ludvík Vaculík, Milan Kundera and Ivan Klíma at the 4th Congress of the Czechoslovak Writers' Union, Prague, 27 June 1967
Credit: CTK Photo/Jovan Dezort

thus all met in Vicky's flat on the housing estate and she offered them every available chair and stool in the place, seating herself on the bed. She did not chair the meetings, and today she was feeling particularly faint, having collected her week's ration two days ago and eaten it all up at a sitting. She had never felt so hungry in her life, and her limbs were growing weaker by the hour. She gazed at these seven alien, useless women, who were discussing meetings, banners, petitions, famine in India, collections of waste material and other, as far as Vicky was concerned, quite incomprehensible topics. Every now and again she felt she was about to doze off, or was she going to faint?

She realised that nothing that was being discussed in her presence affected her in the slightest. None of it would help her get back her fitness, recover her strength, none of it would save her from starving to death.

Opening her eyes with an effort, she saw in front of her the quivering, fleshy nape of the vice-chairwoman. An idea took shape in her always sluggish and now completely exhausted brain. She closed her eyes again, but the idea was still there, as if hovering in front of her, growing increasingly more tempting. Suddenly she became aware that she was swallowing saliva in what seemed to her a loud fashion, but fortunately no one else seemed to have noticed.

Of course, she thought, it can't be the vice-chairwoman, that wouldn't do because who would then chair the meetings? No, she needed the vice-chairwoman. With an access of energy she looked round the room, scanning one of her guests after another. When the meeting was over she went up to the rotund treasurer. 'Could you stay on for a while, comrade? There's something I'd like to discuss with you.'

It was so easy. Her huge hands with their incongruously small fingers were still strong enough to cope with the bones. But the flesh was so tough that she had to use the meat grinder. She had been without proper food for so long now that she could only manage 20 rissoles. Then she went to bed. She could not remember when she had last fallen asleep with such a feeling of well-being. The future suddenly looked rosy again.

The following morning she ate 25 rissoles for breakfast and, for the first time in days, took the ball and her tape measure and went out to train. She threw 21 metres, and the next day improved on that by a full 80 centimetres, the day after that by another metre. She trained hard, running around the wood and, back in her apartment, doing callisthenics and lifting the dumb-bell. On the seventh day her throw measured 29 metres. At the next meeting of the committee she made the treasurer's apologies and asked the secretary if she would kindly stay behind when the others left. On the tenth day she again passed the 30 metre mark. 'Stick it out, Vicky!' she whispered to herself. 'You can do it! You must! It's now or never!'

Within a month the number of committee members was down to three. Fortunately, there was a nasty flu epidemic raging just at that time, so that the good-natured Fighters for Lasting Peace did not become suspicious. The delicious smell of fried meat came incessantly from Vicky's apartment.

Well, just look at that, her neighbours cursed under their breath, they're again giving her special rations! But they had long ago learned not to protest against privileges accorded to others lest they lose what remained of their own, restricted rights.

Vicky now trained like one possessed, giving up all her time to the task. Six weeks after she had resumed her training routine she again threw 40 metres. When she had measured the distance, delighted with what was at last an admirable achievement, she automatically raised her arms in the air and a hoarse cry of triumph came from her lips.

She picked up the ball and the tape-measure and hurried home, for in a few minutes there was to be a meeting of the committee. She would have to move that they co-opt some new members.

To her astonishment, a crowd had gathered outside the entrance, that large, familiar crowd which stared at her with impassioned eyes, obviously restrained only by the efforts of the men in uniform. It did not occur to her to wonder why all these people had gathered there – they could only have come on her account. Now they must have recognised her, for the silence was shattered by a strange, unarticulated roar which grew louder as she approached. And then she saw the clenched fists raised in the air and waving … The roar intensified, and Vicky was once more conscious of that old, almost-forgotten feeling of utter bliss. This pleasurable sensation caused her to shake all over, and her arms flew up in the air. She knew now that she was destined to return to the shot-put circle and to set a new record. At least 45 metres. She could do it! Yes, she could do it! ❐

Translated by George Theiner, former editor of Index on Censorship

©Ivan Klíma
41(2): 128/140
DOI: 10.1177/0306422012447749
www.indexoncensorship.org

Ivan Klíma is an acclaimed writer and former dissident. His many novels include *Love and Garbage* (Random House) and *Waiting for the Dark, Waiting for the Light* (Granta). He has been a regular contributor to *Index* throughout the magazine's history. *Index* was the publisher in London of the Czech dissident journal *Spektrum* in which Klíma and his fellow writers appeared

Free the Word! at Poetry Parnassus

Wed 27 June 2012
The Front Room, Queen Elizabeth Hall Foyer

PEN International, English PEN and the Southbank Centre are hosting a day of free events debating key literary and freedom of expression issues. Visitors will be able to take action on behalf of persecuted writers worldwide and join in fun creative writing workshops.

10:00 – 11:00
PEN International Writers Breakfast – An introduction to PEN's work worldwide
Meet PEN writers and learn more about PEN's role in promoting literature and defending free expression.

11:30 – 12:30
Free The Word! Zones of Conflict – Poets Caught in Global Crisis
Can poets be expected to act as spokespeople in times of crisis? Can poetry provide a suitable form of 'resistance'?

13:00 – 14:00
Free The Word! Exile and Audience
How are writers affected by working in 'dislocation' from their native countries? How does the pressure to remain faithful to heritage whilst embracing the present situation influence literary style?

14:30 – 15:30
Free The Word! Speechless: Minority languages, marginalised voices
What does the future hold for minority literatures in the era of globalisation? Why does linguistic heritage matter to writers now more than ever?

16:00 – 17:00
Free the Word! I Am Not my Country: Antinationalism, borders and identity
What are the problems associated with positioning poets as 'national laureates'? How do borders inform our perspective on poetry as readers?

Poetry Parnassus, part of the London 2012 Festival, is an international celebration of literature, bringing together the world's most exciting poets, rappers, spoken word artists and singers, including Seamus Heaney, Wole Soyinka, John Agard, Shailja Patel, Jack Mapanje and Rafeef Ziadeh.

For more information visit http://www.pen-international.org/ or contact paul.finegan@pen-international.org
International PEN is a registered charity in England and Wales with registration number 1117088

A chronicle of censorship and free expression news in the United Kingdom in 2011 and 2012, incorporating information from the BBC, *Daily Mail, Evening Standard, Guardian,* Huffington Post, *Independent,* journalism.co.uk, Mass High Tech, *Press Gazette,* Reuters, Scottish Parliament, *Sun,* Sense About Science, *Telegraph* and other sources

The High Court ruled that UK internet service providers (ISPs) must block file-sharing website the **Pirate Bay** on 30 April 2012. The Swedish site provides links that enable visitors to download free music and video, which some critics claim to be illegally copied. Several ISPs, including Sky, O2 and Virgin Media had already agreed to block the site. The British Phonographic Industry had asked the same ISPs to voluntarily block access to the site in 2011, but the ISPs refused to do so unless a court order was made. (BBC)

Security guards prevented **five journalists** from photographing and filming the London Olympic Park site on 23 April 2012. Tight regulations on photography are in place inside the sporting complex, but citizens are within their rights to take photographs on public land outside the venue. As the incident, during which camera lenses were physically blocked, took place on public land, the National Union of Journalists warned that security measures should not interfere with media professionals going about their work. (*Guardian*)

On 30 March 2012, the High Court struck out the libel case against **Richard Dawkins Foundation, Amazon.co.uk** and **Vaughan Jones.** Chris McGrath, author of *The Attempted Murder of God: Hidden Science You Really Need to Know,* lodged a libel action in November 2011 after Jones published critical reviews about his book on Amazon in September and October 2010 and a critical article on the Richard Dawkins Foundation website in September 2010. (*Independent,* Sense About Science, *Telegraph*)

On 13 April 2012, London Mayor Boris Johnson blocked an advertising campaign that suggested homosexuality could be cured. The campaign, by Christian group **Core Issues Trust,** mimicked an advert posted on London buses by Stonewall, a group that campaigns for homosexuals' rights. Johnson vetoed the 'offensive' adverts – which read 'Not gay! Ex-gay, post-gay and proud. Get over it!' – a week before they were due to be launched, claiming that the campaign had no place in a tolerant city. (BBC, Huffington Post)

A man from County Antrim, Northern Ireland, was fined £250 on 13 April 2012 for posting abusive, anti-Catholic comments on Facebook in August 2011. **Dean Boyd** told police that he regretted posting the message — which he removed 20 minutes after doing so — but said that the sentiments were intended for his friends to read and he had not aimed to incite hatred. The case was the first prosecution connected with sectarian abuse published on a social networking site in Northern Ireland. (BBC)

Six protesters were arrested in East London on 10 April 2012. Local council officials ordered the protesters, who were part of a larger group demonstrating against the erection of a temporary facility for the 2012 London Olympic Games, to dismantle their camp on Leyton Marsh not far from the site of the summer Games. Members of the **Save Leyton Marsh Group** argued that proper environmental assessments had not been carried out before the building work was approved and that harmful substances could potentially be unearthed when the project commences. (*Guardian*)

On 2 April 2012, Northern Ireland Police took legal steps, via United States authorities, to obtain transcripts of interviews with former IRA members, including an interview with Dolours Price, who played a role in a car bombing in 1973. The transcripts were part of the **Boston College Belfast Project**, a research initiative conducted by academics, historians and journalists that examined the lives and activities of former republicans and loyalists during the Troubles. Researchers for the project believe that releasing the information to the police could risk the lives of people who provided testimonies during the project. The US court hearing was adjourned in order to consider the ruling. (BBC)

Former New Zealand cricket captain Chris Cairns won a High Court libel case on 26 March 2012 after filing a claim in January 2010. Cairns was awarded £90,000 in damages following allegations posted on Twitter that he was involved in match fixing. **Lalit Modi**, former chairman of the Indian Premier League, accused Cairns of having a history of match fixing after being forced to leave the Indian Cricket League in October 2008. The presiding judge stated that there was no evidence that Cairns had been involved in the criminal activity. The case was filed in London, despite the assertion that only 35 readers of the post were from England and Wales; under English libel law, the burden of proof lies with the defendant rather than the plaintiff, making the English courts attractive to those wishing to lodge defamation claims. (BBC)

Azhar Ahmed, of West Yorkshire, appeared before Dewsbury Magistrates Court on 20 March 2012, accused of making 'grossly offensive' comments about the deaths of British soldiers in Afghanistan. Ahmed was charged under the Communications Act 2003 after allegedly posting a message on Facebook about media coverage of British deaths and the comparatively slight coverage of Afghan deaths. The teen also faced a racially-aggravated public order charge, but this was withdrawn. Ahmed, who denied the charges, will stand trial at Huddersfield Magistrates Court on 3 July 2012. (*Daily Mail*)

The Bible Society was refused permission to hand out bibles at the London 2012 Olympics on 15 March 2012 because of Olympic rules regarding the use of the Olympic logo. The group had prepared special Bibles highlighting passages that referred to sport, but the London Organising Committee of the Olympic Games refused to grant the group permission to use the logo as part of their campaign. (*Telegraph*)

A damages claim by Manchester United and Wales footballer Ryan Giggs against the *Sun* newspaper was thrown out by the High Court on 2 March 2012. Giggs was granted an injunction in April 2011 after an article was published in the tabloid about an unnamed player's alleged affair with a model. Until February 2012, an anonymity clause in the injunction made it illegal to name Giggs in print or during parliamentary proceedings, despite the footballer already having been widely identified on Twitter and named in the Commons by an MP in May 2011. Giggs claimed that the tabloid had

'misused' private information and said he was entitled to claim damages for distress and breach of the right to privacy. (*Press Gazette*)

The Scottish government brought into law the amended Offensive Behaviour at Football and Threatening Communications (Scotland) Bill on 1 March 2012, creating two new criminal offences. One relates to **offensive or threatening behaviour** likely to incite public disorder at football matches; the second, 'threatening communications', criminalises recorded exchanges that contain threats of serious violence or threats intended to incite religious hatred. Anyone convicted under the bill faces a maximum of five years' imprisonment. The new laws were introduced as a direct reaction to the escalation of sectarian violence in Scottish football, including parcel bombs being sent to Celtic Manager Neil Lennon, Paul McBride QC and former MSP Trish Godman. The bill was designed to be brought in as emergency legislation at the beginning of the 2011–2012 football season but received harsh criticism and so had to be referred back to the Justice Committee. Free expression advocates expressed concerns that the definition of 'racial hatred' was too broad and that some guidance in the bill is unclear. (*Daily Record*, Scottish Parliament)

Sally Morgan, a professional television psychic, sued the **Daily Mail** newspaper on 26 January 2012 after it published an article entitled 'What a load of crystal balls!'. The article, written by a celebrity magician and former psychic, alleged that Morgan was a charlatan and that the information she presented as part of her programme was obtained via a hidden earpiece. Morgan, who had worked for Princess Diana, claimed the story caused substantial harm to

her reputation and sought damages of £150,000. Morgan also requested an injunction to prevent re-publication of the allegations. (*Press Gazette*)

Media regulator Ofcom revoked the UK licence of Iranian broadcaster Press TV on 21 January 2012. In December 2011, **Press TV** was fined £100,000 for broadcasting a 2009 interview with journalist and filmmaker Maziar Bahari, who was at the time being detained in Evin Prison. Press TV failed to pay the fine. Ofcom also concluded that editorial control of the station rested with the Iranian government in Tehran, a breach of UK broadcasting regulations. (BBC, journalism.co.uk)

Volunteers for the London 2012 Olympics were told they would be subjected to strict rules regarding their use of social media tools during the Games, including a ban on photographs or posts featuring VIPs with special access to non-public sections of the participating venues. The rules for the 70,000 **Games Maker volunteers** were posted on Games Makers' area of the London 2012 Organising Committee's website in early January 2012. The guidelines also appeal to volunteers not to mention details about their role, location or about athletes, celebrities and dignitaries. (BBC)

Police cleared tents from London's Parliament Square after the Police Reform and Social Responsibility Bill came into force on 31 October 2011. **Protesters** had occupied the pavement opposite the Houses of Parliament, nicknamed 'Democracy Village', since May 2010, campaigning on a range of issues. (*Guardian*)

Strictly Come Dancing television personality Nancy Dell'Olio's libel action against the **Daily Mail** was struck out by the High Court on 20

December 2011. Dell'Olio lodged a suit against the tabloid after an article, which was published with the headline 'Return of the man-eater', referred to her relationship with theatre director Sir Trevor Nunn. The article, which was published in April 2011, described Dell'Olio as 'a woman who hunts men'. (*Guardian, Press Gazette*)

An employee was thought to be behind the censorship of various pieces of information provided on **Virgin Media's electronic programme guide** on 20–21 December 2011. Filmmaker Alfred Hitchcock's surname was changed to 'Hitchc**k', musician Jarvis Cocker's surname became 'C**ker', the Premier league football team Arsenal was referred to as 'A**enal' and novelist Charles Dickens's name was also deemed offensive and referred to as 'D**kens'. A Virgin Media spokesperson referred to the profanity checker as 'over-zealous' and the full and correct terms were reinstated shortly after the company realised the mistake. (*Guardian*)

On 12 December 2011, 139 people were arrested in London during a **protest against election results** in the Democratic Republic of Congo. Seven people were charged with offences including obstructing the highway, breaching the Serious Organised Crime and Police Act and an assault on police. (BBC, *Guardian*)

The editor of the *Government and Public Sector Journal*, **Stuart Littleford**, was assaulted by two police officers from Greater Manchester Police on 22 November 2011 after he took photographs of a road accident in Oldham. (*Press Gazette*)

The ban on *This Side Idolatry,* a novel that criticises Charles Dickens, was lifted in Portsmouth on 23 October 2011. The 1929 novel by Carl Roberts offended the City of Portsmouth because it portrayed Dickens, who was born there, unfavourably. The ban was lifted ahead of the 200th anniversary of Dickens's birth and the book was reinstated in libraries. (BBC)

On 19 October 2011, Tesla motors lost a major part of a High Court libel claim against BBC's *Top Gear* television programme. The electric sports car maker sued the BBC after an episode showed the company's Roadster car running out of battery in a race, but the presiding judge said that no viewer would have reasonably compared the car's performance on the show to its performance on a public road. Though the company lost the libel case, it continued to pursue the corporation for malicious falsehood relating to five other statements allegedly made by the presenters about the Roadster. In February 2012, the case for malicious falsehood was also struck out. (*Guardian, Wired*)

Former Smiths front man Morrissey announced his plans to sue *NME*'s former editor **Conor McNicholas** and its publisher, **IPC Media**, for libel in connection with the publication of an interview in which he complained about a loss of British identity as a result of immigration. Morrissey claimed that he suffered reputational damage from the controversial interview he gave the magazine in 2007. Although he was not in court for the hearing on 17 October 2011, Morrissey could be cross-examined before a jury if a trial goes ahead. (**Guardian**)

A Russian property developer who was punched during a talkshow lodged a libel suit in England after his assailant, Russian tycoon **Alexander Lebedev,** said he deserved the attack. Sergei Polonsky sued Lebedev, owner of the *Independent* and London *Evening Standard*, for defamation on 14 October 2011 following the on-screen altercation in September. Criminal proceedings were filed in Russia. (BBC, Reuters)

Following Prime Minister David Cameron's promise to make **online pornography** inaccessible, several internet service providers announced plans to offer parents the option of blocking online content on 11 October 2011. Cameron also launched Parentport, a website hosting parents' reports of inappropriate material. (BBC)

The British Board of Film Classification (BBFC) lifted a ban on horror film *Human Centipede 2* in October 2011, giving it an '18' rating following 32 edits to the film, which had been described as posing a 'real risk of harm' in June 2011. The certification was granted prior to the film's DVD release. (BBC)

On 3 October 2011, Alan Graham demanded that **Rihanna** cover her breasts or leave his farm in Bangor, Northern Ireland. The pop entertainer was filming a music video for her single 'We found love' at his farm in September 2011, which had been hired out for the purpose. Fans of the star in turn verbally attacked the farmer. Graham objected to her filming topless and interrupted filming to complain about her behaviour. (BBC, *Daily Mail*)

Media watchdog Ofcom issued new guidelines regarding the broadcast of explicit **music videos** on 30 September 2011. In an effort to tighten existing nine pm watershed television rules, the guidance focused on visual content of music videos as well as verbal content and was issued after performances from Rihanna and Christina Aguilera during the final episode of the *X Factor* met with thousands of complaints in 2010. Research conducted to support the new guidelines showed that 11% of UK parents were concerned about the airing of music videos before nine pm. (*Guardian*)

Scotland Yard announced on 16 September 2011 that it planned to use the Official Secrets Act (OSA) to force *Guardian* journalists to reveal sources for information about the phone-hacking scandal. The order was described as 'ill-judged' by the newspaper's editor, who spoke out against use of the OSA to undermine the protection of journalists' confidential sources. Metropolitan Police withdrew its plans on 21 September 2011. (*Guardian, Telegraph*)

The Football Association (FA) introduced a code of conduct on 12 September 2011 that aimed to prevent **staff, board and council members from** talking freely to the press. The new 'censorship code' restricts what can be relayed by councillors to bodies they represent and insists that the FA press office be informed about all media enquiries and that no FA business be divulged to the press. The move comes after FA chairman David Bernstein called for a transparent football government in response to reports of corruption in the international football association, Fédération Internationale de Football (Fifa). (*Daily Mail, Telegraph*)

Two men were sentenced to four years' imprisonment for instigating rioting on Facebook on 17 August 2011. **Jordan Blackshaw and Perry Sutcliffe-Keenan** pleaded guilty to using the social networking site to encourage others to cause offence under the Serious Crime Act 2007. (*Guardian*)

On 11 August 2011, Prime Minister David Cameron announced that the government was exploring ways of **banning individuals** from using **social networking sites** if they are thought to be using them to organise criminal activity. The announcement followed reports that the BlackBerry Messenger service was used to organise riots in London in early August. Cameron stated that the home secretary would meet with representatives from Facebook, Twitter and Research In Motion to discuss the companies' roles in controlling use of media tools; he added that broadcasters also had a responsibility to supply footage of the riots to police. Similar requests had met with resistance in the past, as broadcasters asserted their right to maintain editorial independence. (*Guardian*)

In June 2011, the European Union announced that it would not be screening a film it had funded. The film, made in late 2010 by Clementine Malpas, looks at the lives of Afghan women in prison for 'moral crimes'. EU spokespeople insisted that the identities of the women featured in the film, *In-Justice: The Story of Afghan Women*, were not protected and that their lives could potentially be endangered. Malpas insisted that the women featured had decided to take part in the film and so deserved to have their voices heard. (al Arabiya, *Evening Standard*)

Google was asked to remove 135 **YouTube videos** in the first six months of 2011. The takedown requests were believed to be in connection with perceived threats to UK national security. Figures published by Google, YouTube's owner, showed a 71% rise in content removal requests from the UK government or police. The videos were removed following complaints about privacy, security and hate speech. (*Guardian*)

On 20 May 2011, a committee investigating the rise of superinjunctions and anonymised privacy injunctions emphasised the need for open justice and public hearings. Lord Neuberger, Master of the Rolls, formed the committee in April 2010 in response to widespread concern about **secret injunctions**, whose very existence cannot be reported. The committee, which reported its findings at the Royal Courts of Justice, made a number of procedural recommendations, such as the creation of a secure database tracking injunctions and drafted guidance for injunction applications. The new procedure, the committee said, would enable the media to be informed about applications in advance. (Index on Censorship)

Former Fédération Internationale de l'Automobile (FIA) chief Max Mosley failed in his bid to impose a legal duty of **'prior notification' on the press** on 10 May 2011. Mosley lodged a case at the European Court of Human Rights after UK newspaper the *News of the World* published details of his sex life. Victory for Mosley could have meant that media outlets would have been required to contact subjects of stories prior to publication; there were fears that such a step would lead to a rise in interim injunctions barring publication. (Index on Censorship, journalism.co.uk)

In 2011, a series of **injunctions and superinjunctions** were ordered to prevent the media from reporting news about the private lives of celebrities and high profile figures.

On 19 May, it was disclosed in the House of Lords that a judge granted anonymity to a claimant in a libel case concerning former banker Sir Fred Goodwin. On 26 April, news emerged that journalist and broadcaster Andrew Marr obtained a superinjunction to prevent reporting of an extra-marital affair in 2008. Also in April, media outlets were prevented from naming the premiership footballer involved with model Imogen Thomas. (BBC, *Independent, Telegraph*)

In a landmark judgment on 3 May 2011, the High Court ruled that the Metropolitan Police acted illegally towards **protesters** who staged demonstrations against the G20 summit on 1 April 2009. The court heard that officers used a range of violent tactics against protesters, many of whom police chiefs accepted were demonstrating in a peaceful manner. The police were also found guilty of 'kettling', a crowd control strategy that restrains large groups in a confined area for extended periods of time. **Josh Moos and Hannah McClure** brought the case against the police after they were among a crowd of up to 5000 held for five hours. (*Guardian*)

After launching a series of libel cases against cardiologist **Peter Wilmshurst** that continued for close to five years, US company NMT Medical announced on 20 April 2011 that it was ceasing operations. One of the cases lodged by NMT followed Wilmshurst's criticism of clinical trials of a heart device manufactured by NMT Medical and another pertained to comments he made on BBC Radio 4's *Today* programme. (*Guardian, Press Gazette*, Sense About Science)

In March 2011, former Member of Scottish Parliament Tommy Sheridan attempted to prevent the publication of ***Tommy Sheridan: From Hero to Zero?***, a biography that alleged that he degraded women during his early political career. Sheridan threatened to sue the author, Professor Gregor Gall, who had refused to send Sheridan a copy of the manuscript before it was published. (*Herald*)

Edited by Natasha Schmidt
Compiled by Alice Purkiss
DOI 10.1177/0306422012448288

CULTURE CRUSH

Writers in protest from India
and Sri Lanka

Index archive: Judy Blume
and Ivan Kraus

Celebrations marking the end of Sri Lanka's civil war, Colombo, 19 May 2009
Credit: David Gray/Reuters

TAKING A STAND

As literary festivals and fairs become forums of censorship and protest, **Salil Tripathi** considers the challenges facing writers and their readers

There are many ways to protest against a writer whose views or work you dislike. You can close the book, as novelist Salman Rushdie once proposed in a speech in India in 2010. You can write a book to counter the arguments with which you disagree, as Indian peace activist Maulana Wahiduddin Khan suggested to Muslims who strongly opposed *The Satanic Verses*. You can tell others how awful the writer's work is, so that they don't make the mistake of buying it. You can even picket an event where the writer is scheduled to speak, letting the audience know your views.

What you should not do in a free society is force the organisers to cancel the invitation to the writer, intimidate publishers so that they don't dare to print the book, or threaten the writer, his supporters and his audience with violence.

And yet, in January this year, in what is now billed as the world's largest literary festival in Jaipur, India, Muslim groups succeeded on every front in a protest against the presence of Salman Rushdie. In 1988, a few self-appointed politicians claiming to speak for India's millions of Muslims warned the Indian government of the mayhem that lay ahead if *The Satanic Verses* was imported or published in India. The government acquiesced and imposed an import ban; Penguin India, which had the Indian rights to publish the novel, decided not to print the edition in India at all. Nearly a quarter century later, the *darululoom* of Deoband, a seminary that trains conservative Muslim preachers, told the organisers of the Jaipur literary festival that they should not have invited Rushdie. The festival stood firm, until Rushdie decided to pull out: he had received what appeared to be credible warnings from the state police that a hit squad was on its way. The threat turned out to be a hoax.

Then the festival organisers did something odd. When four authors – first, US-based Amitava Kumar and Hari Kunzru, and later, India-based Ruchir Joshi and Jeet Thayil – read out passages from *The Satanic Verses,* the festival intervened to stop their protest. Police officers stepped in and questioned them. The festival also issued a statement distancing itself from the writers, as though they had done something shameful or wrong.

The organisers then tried to retrieve the festival's central purpose, and decided to conduct a live conversation with Rushdie via video-link. But the Muslim protesters, once appeased, wanted more; they threatened again, saying they would demonstrate at the festival and would not be held responsible for the consequences. High drama followed, and the owner of the palace where the festival takes place pulled the plug, refusing to allow the video-link to proceed. Ironically, Rushdie then got an audience of millions, as he spoke to Indian journalist Barkha Dutt from London on television within an hour of the cancellation, multiplying his audience. Meanwhile, several political activists belonging to all major parties filed lawsuits against the four writers, saying that their act intended to cause public unrest and hurt sensibilities.

There was more than one redeeming outcome however. A group of writers circulated a petition in Jaipur calling for the lifting of the ban on *The Satanic Verses*. Delhi-based critic and writer Nilanjana Roy was one of the prime movers behind it. She thinks India has two models of literary festival – one based on the *durbar*, and one on the open *math*, or field. The *durbar* festival celebrates literary pomp, but is uncomfortable with genuinely subversive or revolutionary discussion; the open *math* encourages free expression of all kinds, providing a space outside the control of the state. 'It is very different from the polite and ultimately unthreatening views of drawing-room conversations,' she says. Reflecting on Jaipur, she adds: 'What we saw there was the *durbar* reaction – it wasn't just that the organisers distanced themselves, laying down rules for what can and can't be said at an apparently open literary event, but that they reflected the Indian middle-class discomfort with dissent. Festivals are hollow spectacles if they can't protect

Muslims shout slogans against Salman Rushdie, who cancelled his appearance
at the Jaipur Literature Festival because of threats, 20 January 2012
Credit: Altaf Hussain/Reuters

what is truly important – the free movement of words and ideas. If they set up border posts where an idea has to go through security checks before it can be articulated, you don't have a literary festival, though you may still have a grand literary circus.'

Two months after the Jaipur fiasco, Rushdie came to New Delhi and spoke at a conclave organised by a magazine. He said pretty much what he wanted to about pretty much everything.

A literary festival is above all an exchange of ideas. The ideas may be deplorable to some, inspiring to others; controversial to one group, affirming to another. A festival that does not permit room for ideas, for debate, becomes a monologue, or, as Roy puts it, a circus; it is no longer a conversation.

There is of course an element of spectacle, of theatre in a literary festival – the grand entry, the large screen, the panel, the attractive presenters, the music programmes, the cocktail parties, and the autograph-signing sessions. A writer in front of an audience, expressing his or her view, can have an electrifying effect; a spirited debate between writers, or writers and readers, can be a memorable experience.

The instinct of the organisers at Jaipur was right – to create space where doubts can be raised and ideas challenged. But when the crunch came, the festival caved into groups threatening violence while the state abdicated its responsibilities, failing to stand by the four writers who protested. The festival could not force Rushdie to come, and Rushdie had good reason not to come; nor could the organisers prevail upon the owner of the palace, or the security forces, to provide sufficient protection to a peaceful audience which had gathered to listen to a writer. The organisers themselves have since also been targeted in lawsuits filed by activists from Muslim groups and political parties.

While outwardly a democracy, India's constitutional guarantees of free speech place several limits, such as restricting speech that may incite violence, offend others, or promote religious hatred. Two specific sections in its criminal laws grant the state the power to prosecute anyone who misuses his right to speak freely, as well as giving any individual who claims to have been offended by a particular speech or piece of writing the right to lodge a criminal complaint.

Authors in Sri Lanka have faced a different pressure – the call to boycott. This issue came into focus last year, when many writers, including Arundhati Roy, called upon invited authors to boycott the Galle literary festival in Sri Lanka, as a mark of protest against the brutal manner in which the army annihilated the Tamil Tigers and killed tens of thousands of civilians during the last phase of the civil war. In the end, only a few writers complied with the boycott. The debate over Galle became emotionally charged, as Tamil and other human rights activists quite rightly condemned the Sri Lankan government over the way it conducted the war. Is it even possible to have a dialogue with a government accused of crimes against humanity?

Michigan-based novelist V V Ganeshananthan has thought long and hard about this issue. She wrote a moving novel, *Love Marriage,* about a family from the Tamil diaspora and its relationship with the country. She decided to participate in the festival in 2009 before the final onslaught in the civil war. It was a bold decision, and she wrote an eloquent essay arguing against a boycott on the website www.themillions.com, where she said: 'The great traditions of solidarity are built on conversation, long and careful study and thought, and yes, informed travel of the mind and body – not the petition of a moment. This is a long engagement, and must emphasise serious exchange – something that has no chance of happening if the door is closed.'

Galle Literary Festival participants and attendees were encouraged to share artwork and comments on the festival's graffiti wall, Galle, Sri Lanka, 29 January 2010
Credit: Dinuka Liyanawatte/Reuters

Reflecting on the festival three years later, she says: 'It is hard to make absolute arguments – the politics of each festival and state are particular, and should be looked at that way – but if a festival did not provide real room for opposition and argument, and if activists in the country advocated a boycott, I would consider it. Thus far, that hasn't been the case in Galle. Many activists have worked or participated there. A number of people involved in its organisation are critical of multiple actors in Sri Lankan politics.' She is aware that she is herself part of the Tamil diaspora, which is regularly criticised in the Sri Lankan media. 'By going to Galle, I provide something of a counter-narrative: the diaspora isn't a faceless monolith, and it has its own varied and complicated stories. I also have the opportunity to be in conversation with an audience that's actively seeking out new ideas about literature and politics. I want Sri Lanka to be in conversation with the world beyond its shores – and just as importantly, vice versa.'

China offers an even bigger challenge. It hosts literary festivals, and some writers have questioned whether an open dialogue there is even possible. Tina Mani Kanagaratnam, co-director of the Shanghai International Literary Festival and the Capital Literary Festival Beijing, which she has been running for a decade, says: 'Increased openness is a journey. It does not come from freezing out countries, it comes from engagement – yes, on their terms – and it comes slowly, but it comes. We are well-behaved guests in China, and we give controversy a wide berth. But within our festival, we do have discussions and dialogue, and that dialogue helps us understand each other, and share why each of our value sets are so important to us. That is a key point: China and the west need to understand each other, and not have one dictate what "universal values" are to the other. No, we don't ever have a writer that would be considered controversial, because that would mean getting shut down, and at the end of the day, being engaged is much more important than turning our backs in protest. To turn our backs, even in the name of principle, is to turn our backs on Chinese writers too.'

But what about London? Should Britain crowd out criticism? China was this year's 'market focus' at the London Book Fair, which is a trade fair. British publishers want access to the Chinese market, and Chinese authors would like wider recognition. But which Chinese authors? The invited list of authors at this year's festival was approved by the Chinese government, which inevitably meant that authors who have defied censorship in China, or who have been imprisoned for questioning the Party's authority, were absent. Authors such as Jung Chang and Ma Jian, who live abroad but have written critically about China, were not part of the official delegation. In contrast, when India was the market focus a few years ago, several Indian authors based in the United States or Britain were part of the official programme.

There is a word in Mandarin – *zige* – which can be loosely translated as standing, or worth. The Asia scholar Ian Buruma points out in his thoughtful book about Chinese dissidents, *Bad Elements,* the Chinese government characterises activists and writers who leave China as figures who have lost their standing. By not including Jung Chang and Ma Jian in the pantheon of contemporary Chinese writers, the Chinese government was delegitimising them.

Ma contests the government's standing on this issue. The London-based author of *Beijing Coma*, the epic novel about the Chinese nation's stultification after the Tiananmen Square massacre in 1989, opposed the presence of officially approved Chinese authors at the London Book Fair this year. Many human rights and literary organisations expressed

Protests at the London Book Fair, where China was the 'market focus', 17 April 2012
Credit: Robert Sharp

disappointment, in particular over the British Council agreeing with the Chinese authority's choice of writers. English PEN, which invites speakers attending the fair each year at its literary cafe, invited only one official delegate whose work it had supported in the past and pointedly hosted Jung Chang at its cafe. Its director, Jonathan Heawood, said: 'There are more Chinese writers in detention than are included in the official programme at the London Book Fair. That's why we can't endorse this programme by uncritically hosting these authors. However, we are looking forward to meeting all the writers who are coming, and to debating free expression and literature in China. We want to engage with Chinese authors, but we do not want to endorse the Chinese regime.' It is always a challenge, and the truth is nuanced. Just as it is mindless to boycott every government with a poor human rights record, it is equally thoughtless to engage with every government uncritically. If a hypothetical festival in apartheid-era South Africa prevented black South African writers from participating, then invited international writers – black or white – would be expected to boycott such a festival. If a festival was organised by a government accused of genocide, writers would again be expected to stay away. Should a writer use such opportunities to shame those with power?

Hari Kunzru, who read from Rushdie's novel in India and now faces charges there, says: 'The important point is that freedom of speech is only defended by exercising it. Asserting the value of freedom of expression in the abstract is all very well, but you only find out who's genuinely committed when you actually say something controversial or transgressive. In between the sterile politics of cultural boycott and the equally sterile politics of uncritical "engagement" is a space where you can force power to speak – that's the crucial point here. Power would always rather remain silent and invisible. Forcing it to reveal itself is a powerful political act.'

Such acts have consequences, and brave writers, for centuries, have spoken truth to power. ❐

©Salil Tripathi
41(2): 151/158
DOI: 10.1177/0306422012448150
www.indexoncensorship.org

Salil Tripathi is a journalist and regular contributor to *Index*

Index on Censorship

Celebrating **40 years of the world's best authors, artists and thinkers**

As the world's most influential free expression magazine, Index on Censorship is a must read for free thinkers everywhere. For 40 years, it has reported on free expression violations, published banned writing and given a voice to those who have been prevented from speaking out.

From freedom of information and state control of the internet to whistleblowing and jokes on Twitter, free expression is one of today's most challenging issues and something that affects us all. Through challenging and intelligent analysis, Index on Censorship sets the agenda for the most urgent free expression issues of the day.

Take advantage of our 40% discount on print subscriptions to celebrate 40 years of Index in Censorship

Margaret Atwood **Isaac Babel Daniel Barenboim Samuel Beckett** Mikhail Bulgakov **William Boyd** Noam Chomsky **Ariel Dorfman Shirin Ebadi Umberto Eco** Harold Evans **Nadine Gordimer**

www.indexoncensorship.org/subscribe

US and Latin America

Responding to George Theiner's 'Opinion' piece in Index on Censorship 2/1985, Mr Elliott Abrams, the US Assistant Secretary of State, writes:

I agree completely that *Index* is a rare opportunity for writers from countries that are not free to tell the world about their problems. Indeed, this is one of the key roles of your publication. Certainly, many of those whose works appear in *Index* have a great deal of trouble being heard in their own countries. If these people express anti-American views, that is no fault of yours, and it would be wrong to criticise you or to suggest that you censor the authentic views of writers whose whole problem is precisely the existence of censorship.

However, the remarks of which I complained were *not* those of a suppressed Haitian intellectual unable to appear in print in Port-au-Prince. They were those of a free Western intellectual, who one assumes does not suffer from the problem of government oppression. I would have had no complaint had a Haitian writer made an anti-American remark, much as I might disagree with it; my complaint was about your author, and I am gratified that you seem to agree that the sentences I mentioned were gratuitous political rhetoric.

I am afraid that you yourself fall into the same trap in your statement. There you say 'It is an inescapable fact that the policies adopted by the US in Central and South America for many decades — with their stubborn support of brutal dictatorships such as those of Batista, Somoza, Stroessner and Pinochet — have resulted in much anti-American feeling in that part of the world'.

May I suggest to you that the term 'an inescapable fact' is hardly applicable to your description of American policy toward the dictatorships mentioned as 'stubborn support'. Two of the four are in power today. To take Paraguay first, I believe you are mistaken in suggesting that there is widespread anti-American feeling there. The US Embassy is the most active one in that country on human rights questions, and maintains constant and close contact with opponents of President Stroessner. I meet with Paraguayan dissidents regularly, and as you would expect, some think the US position is fine and others think we need to do more (while acknowledging that many, especially the Europeans, do nothing). It is exceptional to meet Paraguayan dissidents unaware of American human rights activities in Paraguay, and I have never once met one

NEWS & NOTES

who believed that our attitude toward the Stroessner regime was 'stubborn support'.

Similarly in Chile, though the situation there is not as clear cut. The Chilean dissidents with whom I meet ask for more US activism, but again I know of none in the Christian Democratic or Socialist parties who believe that our attitude toward Pinochet is 'stubborn support'. In the last six months we have made 15 official denunciations of human rights violations in Chile; which government has made more? This year we refused to support a loan for Chile in the World Bank and one in the Inter-American Development Bank, on human rights grounds. We were alone in taking these positions; the Latin and European votes were for the loans.

I hope my point is clear. You did not have Chileans or Paraguayans stating the 'inescapable fact' that America's policy today is one of 'stubborn support' for Stroessner and Pinochet; instead, *you* made that comment. Here again, I could not possibly object to the genuine views of oppressed writers in either of those countries, for it is your purpose quite rightly to give them an opportunity to speak. But I feel completely justified in objecting when the voices that express anti-American feelings or analyses are not those of oppressed writers, but those of European intellectuals often far from the scene about which they claim to know 'inescapable facts'. ∎

Hide the books

Andrew Graham-Yooll, writing in the April *London Magazine* recalls one of Costa Rica's publishers telling him: 'If you are travelling to Guatemala we can make an invoice of books with innocuous names, sir. Otherwise hide them, or rip off the covers. Border guards do not read, sir, they are just told to look at the covers.' ∎

Refugees' story

Out of the Ashes is a richly-illustrated 48-page booklet on the 1½ million refugees from El Sàlvador and Guatemala. It emphasises how the refugees, fleeing what is often government-inspired violence, are building new communities in the camps of Honduras and Mexico, and preparing themselves for the return to their own countries. It is largely left to the refugees to tell their own story, in poems, songs, statements and letters.

'We want a country where all of us have food and a house to live in, where no-one will die of hunger, of misery, exploitation; where all will have access to medicine, and bodies are no longer dumped in the street.' *Out of the Ashes* available at £2.50 + 40p postage from El Salvador Committee for Human Rights, 20 Compton Terrace, London 2UN. ∎

New law

The Brazilian Ministry of Justice has set up a commission to reform the laws governing censorship now that Brazil has a civilian president and the laws of national security have been repealed. The commission, led by journalist Pompeu de Souza, includes songwriter Chico Buarque (whose songs were censored for a long time in the early 1970s, and who figures in *Index* 4/1979 p 47), the cartoonist Ziraldo, the film director Ana Carolina and the actresses Marília Pera and Lélia Sfat. As a first step, the commission proposed that all works censored since 1964 should be made freely available. They are thought to be considering which would replace the political and moral concerns, on which previous legislation was based, with an age classification for films and a categorisation of TV programmes according to the time they are shown. The commission has already run into criticism that it is too narrowly based, having no television or radio experts and no members of the public. ∎

Taiwan *tangwai*

At the end of April the authorities launched a new campaign, known as 'Chung Hsing' to 'clean up' opposition publications. More than 1,000 plain-clothes and uniformed policemen took part in this campaign. Printers, distributors and news-stands which sell opposition publications have been systematically raided, and their publications seized. These are mainly Taiwanese *tangwai* ('outside the party', outside the ruling Kuomintang Party) 1949) publications and include magazines issued by members of the National Assembly.

As reported in the last issue of *Index* (3/1985, page 44), a high-level government officials held on 17 October 1984 decided to intensify the suppression of 'thought pollution', 'sedition' and 'illegal opinions'. Some of these 'illegal opinions' reveal the involvement of top officials of the Military Intelligence Bureau of the Ministry of Defence in the planning of the assassination of Henry Liu, a Chinese-American journalist and author, in California in October

A SIMPLE SOLUTION

Ivan Kraus wrote an open letter to Romanian leader Nicolae Ceausescu with some tips for keeping better tabs on his citizens

Dear Mr Ceausescu,

I have for some time now been following your political career with great admiration because I know that you alone decide what is and what isn't good for Romania. This in an age when in many countries politicians still waste a lot of time by indulging in lengthy and fruitless debates in parliaments and legislative assemblies. I'm therefore convinced it is no exaggeration to say that there is no statesman in the world today who would show so personal an interest in his citizens as you do.

I have just learned about your latest measures from the daily press. Having ascertained that the Romanians eat too much and that, as a result, a full third of the population suffers from diseases due to obesity, you have proposed a diet consisting of ten eggs, ten dekagrams of butter and a kilogram of meat per citizen per month. You have also decreed that room temperatures should not exceed 15 degrees Celsius, being well aware that citizens of a socialist state must not be too delicate. Your order that lifts should only operate from the third floor up will likewise help to improve the physical fitness of your people, just as the decision not to use refrigerators in winter and to switch the TV off at 10pm every night, except on special occasions such as the days when the nation is celebrating a birthday – yours, your wife's, or that of some other member of your family.

It is to be regretted that some of your citizens seem not to understand the wisdom of these measures you have decided to take, so that it is necessary for the police to step in and keep a watchful eye to make sure that people don't overheat their homes, use their fridges in winter, or consume too much energy on illumination, cooking, ironing, or watching TV. It is only the irresponsible attitude of a few individuals that makes it necessary to resort to blocking up their points.

Bucharest, 31 December 1989
Credit: NAF Dementi

I, however, am an optimist and believe that before too long everyone will realise that they can only hope to see a brighter tomorrow if today they switch the lights off early. It is no secret that you and all your family have to work very hard. Your son Nicu is minister for youth, your brothers Ion and Ilie are in charge of the Ministries of Planning and Defence respectively, another brother, Nicolae, heads the Ministry of the Interior. Moreover, your wife is your first deputy.

It is well known that altogether 50 members of your family have to devote all their time, energy and talents to the job of running Romania, with its 22 million inhabitants. That makes it almost half a million citizens per member of your family, and that is a record that cannot be equalled anywhere in the world today. Not even Flick in West Germany, Heineken in Holland, Grundig or Ford can measure up to you in effectiveness. Duvalier achieves only minimal output with his employees, Idi Amin has gone bankrupt, and Khomeini has too many shareholders and still cannot make a go of it.

I mention all this only because I think that your latest idea – to register all typewriters in the country – requires a little more elaboration. Allow me therefore to discuss this interesting measure and to make a few suggestions as to how it could be improved.

First of all, it is absolutely essential also to register chalks, pens, crayons, pencils, brushes, as well as ink, varnishes and sprays (insofar as these are obtainable in your country), and other material such as paper, notepads and exercise books. And talking about paper, you mustn't forget wrapping and toilet paper. Also all kinds of material used to cut out, stick on or otherwise position letters of the alphabet. I am referring to newspapers, sacks, textiles, scissors, glues, drawing pins, needles, pins and nails.

However, people can use other means too to express anti-State or otherwise harmful sentiments. By means of the Morse code, for example, which can be transmitted with the aid of light. For that reason I would recommend the registration of lamps, chandeliers, torches, bulbs, batteries, spotlights, lanterns, fireworks, as well as mirrors. More primitive methods such as smoke signals can also be used to convey anti-State slogans, for which reason I would restrict the sale of matches, candles, lighters, as well as cigars and cigarettes.

Furthermore, you must not forget all the objects that can be used to transmit sound signals. No citizen should thus be in a position to obtain without permit bells, whistles, and musical instruments (percussion, wind and string – for short distances). The number of musical instruments owned by all orchestras and ensembles should be checked without delay, and reliable musicians issued with music passports.

All this, however, is still not enough. People wishing to express some anti-State thought can be extremely ingenious, as I discovered in Prague in 1968, when the arrival of Soviet troops gave rise to what I might call a festival of anti-State creativity. The lesson we learned then was that citizens can make use of empty tins, dustbins, boxes, barrels, as well as tyres and building materials such as bricks, breeze blocks, beams and planks. Tools to be found in any storeroom must also be included in this category: pliers, picks, hoes, shovels, drills, scythes, even sickles.

Furniture, too, can come in handy. All you need is a few tables, chairs, hat stands, benches or wardrobes and you can put together a slogan. Nor should farmers and farm labourers be left out. They can achieve the same result with the aid of sugarbeet, potatoes, marrows, any kind of vegetable and also all larger – ie legible – species of fruit. Even the smaller fruits, such as redcurrants, blueberries and raspberries, can be made use of for writing, if not on walls, then certainly on tables. Similarly, pots and pans, saucepans, lids, plates, in short all kitchen utensils, crockery and even cutlery offer similar possibilities.

And, alas, we cannot exclude medicine bottles and pills, including vitamins, while foodstuffs too can be misused. Sausages, salamis, hams, loaves of bread, rolls, butter, yoghurt, ice cream, beer and other bottles – all this is potential communication material, just as various personal items such as lipsticks, compacts, make-up kits, purses, watches, and chewing gum.

Finally, I must draw your attention to yet another object – the book. Or rather books. I know that these are carefully censored before they ever get to the bookshops, libraries, schools or scientific institutes. But it is not their content which concerns me here. The very shape of a book makes it an ideal tool for the compiling of words or whole sentences, so that all an inventive anti-State person needs, for instance, is a pile of your own, ideologically absolutely innocuous autobiographies, or some other officially sanctioned works, from which to compose an unsuitable slogan.

I am well aware that any systematic measures to prevent the spreading of anti-State ideas in the way I have outlined above would be extremely costly. I realise that it would require the appointment of special censors in every office, factory, institute and cooperative. They would also have to be sent to other sectors, such as the railways, road transport, and district and regional administration, and above all every street and house. Not to mention the armed forces and the police.

If I take into account the cost of the reporting and systematic registration of all individual objects, to which has to be added the expense incurred in setting up and operating the central censorship offices and control commissions, it occurs to me – as I sit here typing on what is as yet a free, unregistered typewriter – that there would be a far simpler and cheaper solution, which I take the liberty of offering for your consideration. I suggest that we solve the problem rationally and simply by abolishing the alphabet. That is the only way we can achieve socialism quickly and without risk. ❑

©Ivan Kraus
41(1): 160/165
DOI: 10.1177/0306422012438658
www.indexoncensorship.org

Ivan Kraus is a Czech writer and satirist. This article first appeared in *Index on Censorship* Volume 14, Number 4, August 1985

Effigy of Ceausescu, Bucharest, January 1990

REUTERS/Arko Datt

TRUSTLAW

EMPOWERING PEOPLE THROUGH INFORMATION

Looking for high-impact pro bono opportunities in your country or elsewhere? Or free legal assistance?

Interested in the latest on women's rights and corruption worldwide?

TrustLaw is a free global service designed to make it simpler for lawyers to engage in pro bono work and easier for NGOs and social entrepreneurs to access free legal assistance.

TrustLaw is also a global hub of news and information on good governance, anti-corruption and women's rights from our correspondents and content partners. The site includes articles, blogs, case studies, multimedia and country profiles.

trust.org/trustlaw

THOMSON REUTERS FOUNDATION

NOW AVAILABLE FROM SEAGULL BOOKS

MANIFESTOS FOR THE 21ST CENTURY

EDITED BY URSULA OWEN AND JUDITH VIDAL-HALL

IN COLLABORATION
WITH INDEX ON CENSORSHIP

TRUST
MONEY, MARKETS AND SOCIETY
GEOFFREY HOSKING
HB, 100PP, $14.95 / £9.50

HUMANITARIAN ASSISTANCE?
HAITI AND BEYOND
NEIL MIDDLETON
HB, 100PP, $14.95 / £9.50

THAT'S OFFENSIVE
CRITICISM, IDENTITY, RESPECT
STEFAN COLLINI
HB, 76PP, $14.95 / £9.50

WHO DO YOU THINK YOU ARE?
THE SEARCH FOR ARGENTINA'S LOST CHILDREN
ANDREW GRAHAM-YOOLL
HB, 110PP, $14.95 / £9.50

HISTORY THIEVES
ZINOVY ZINIK
HB, 120PP, $14.95 / £9.50

Seagull BOOKS

LONDON NEW YORK CALCUTTA
www.seagullbooks.org

TRADE ENQUIRIES TO UPM, 0117 9020275
DISTRIBUTED BY JOHN WILEY, 1243 779777
FOR THE UNIVERSITY OF CHICAGO PRESS
www.press.uchicago.edu

POEMS FROM THE EDGE

Frances Harrison reports on poetry from both sides of Sri Lanka's bloody civil war, capturing the trauma of a devastating conflict

In 2009, decades of ethnic conflict in Sri Lanka officially ended in an orgy of violence. The International Red Cross called it 'an unimaginable human catastrophe', the United Nations a 'bloodbath'. Hundreds of thousands of civilians were bombed, shelled, starved and denied proper medical care – punished by the government for their support of an armed Tamil rebellion.

It now seems possible 40,000 minority Tamils perished on white sand tropical beaches in the space of just five months, making Sri Lanka one of the bloodiest wars so far this century.

Eyewitnesses describe children in the war zone having their limbs amputated without anaesthetic in hospitals that smelled like butchers' shops, and people being blown up in front of them as they fled to escape the shells.

When the guns went silent on 18 May 2009, exuberant Sinhalese from the majority community poured onto the streets, waving flags and letting off firecrackers, oblivious to the loss of life. Soldiers exchanged trophy photographs of half-naked dead women's bodies and the rebel leader's corpse – pictures that swiftly appeared online.

All the exhausted, traumatised Tamil survivors were herded into squalid refugee camps – supposedly for security reasons. Thousands bribed their way out, fearing rape, torture or disappearance if they remained. Everyone who walked out of the war zone alive had cheated death. The number of amputations and injuries was staggering even for aid workers used to war. Many children were separated from their parents in the rush to escape, others orphaned.

Never had Sri Lanka's two main communities been so far apart. For years they had been divided by language, with some young Tamils growing up in areas of the north of the island controlled by the Tamil Tiger rebels without ever meeting a Sinhalese civilian. Even if they had met, they would have required a translator.

This makes it all the more surprising that Tamil and Sinhalese poets have both been writing – in isolation from one another – about the catastrophe that occurred in their divided island in 2009.

Much of the poetry expresses views that cannot be published inside Sri Lanka. Sinhalese who criticise the military solution to the conflict have been threatened, silenced or hounded out. Many of the country's top journalists have gone into exile. Anyone who raises the issue of war crimes is denounced as a traitor. Tackling the subject of rape is particularly sensitive. While the army denies the use of rape as a weapon of war, the situation of survivors is made even worse by the powerful stigma in Tamil society. Very few women will come forward and admit to having been sexually abused for fear of rejection by their own families, with the result that they often try to commit suicide as the only way out of their predicament.

The Tamil poetry of Elil Rajan is raw, jagged and dripping with fresh horror. Rajan is a Jesuit priest, who has faced criticism from his peers for writing graphically about sexual abuse. Priests and nuns in Sri Lanka hear first-hand about the horror of rape because they are some of the few people the victims will confide in afterwards. 'It's difficult to explain rape as it happened,' he says. 'I do it in poetry through metaphor.' The imagery includes the symbol of a woman to denote both the Tamil motherland and the individual – raped literally and figuratively by the Sinhala soldiers.

As a Tamil, Elil Rajan was first displaced by the war at the age of 11. Knowing from experience what it's like to be a refugee, he wrote this poem about a Tamil child in the government detention camp at the end of the war:

Tamil refugee camp, Vavuniya, Sri Lanka, 26 May 2009
Credit: Sipa Press/Rex Features

> The child lies in the hot sun
> The dust in his eyes
> Sweat trickles down his ribs
> And collects in his hollow stomach
> As starvation.

To see once prosperous farmers reduced to begging for food and water rather than demanding their political rights was shocking:

> A hungry hand stretches out
> It's neither his nor hers
> Reduced from people to
> Just pots and pans
> Fighting for food

(continues on page 179)

May 18th

Black July
Black May
Everything looks dark
White hope has faded
People wear black clothes
And our faces disappear in the darkness of mourning
Along with all traces of our identity.
Demonstrations do not give any hope
Because we've become the greedy Lion's prey
Now we ourselves have even prostituted Freedom
In order to wear rich clothes
The rape will continue until the Lion's lust abates
And there's nothing else left.
Every year we will mourn
And write in our history books of mass murder
We will say that Tamils are all gone
Chased away from our land

Because of those traitors ready to betray Freedom
Resurrection is not for us
The dove is alive but
Drinking the blood produced in Mullivaikkal.

Elil Rajau

Broken Pottu Poem

'Many thousands of the children in the camps have lost both their parents'
News from the Sri Lankan 'welfare camps' – 2009

Bright red pottu
Every morning
Never missed.
The point of your finger
Right here between our eyebrows
For both of us.
Amma [Mummy] puts hers first
Then she puts mine.
Remember me insisting
Me first, me first!

That day Dad give me a biggest hug, squeezed so tight,
Lifted me so high, laughing so loud.
At midnight he went out of the bunker.
Amma must have known he wasn't coming back
But still she smiled at me.

The day she went out of the bunker
Her pottu was still shining between her eyebrows.
Then her pottu went right into her head
And red blood came all down her calm, loving face.

Before then I only knew how to cry.
Then I knew how to shriek, to scream
Holding on to your body, Amma,

Scream!
Scream!
Scream!

Here too our school is under the trees
But they don't take the register.
I don't mind, I'm used to it.

The only thing different is
There are no bunkers here.
Sometimes my heart beats so hard
It's louder than the gunshots
And tears just shoot out when I think about you.

Please don't ask me about pottu
If Amma can't put it on me I don't want it.
And please don't teach us about parents,
I don't want to hear about them.
It's not only me; none of us want to hear it.

July 2009
Mahesh Munsinghe
Translated by Prasanna Ratnayake

The Emperor's Clothes

Do not question
the numbers
when speaking of
your dead sons
in the field of war.
accept quietly
your death dues.
Hush! Don't worry!
just in case
you trouble
Our Army Officers.

Gentlemen of the Black Robes,
you who were called traitors,
we know your Glory!
Hush! Shut your ears!
No Legal Action against
The Power Holders now
just in case
you distress
Their Leader.

A billion ends with nine zeros!
war is indeed costly
on what, pray, was it all spent?
Hush! No questions please!
Just in case
you embarrass
Our Rulers.

The liberated are free
in detention camps,
should another
Liberator descend to
free them.
Hush, Make no noise!
just in case
Our Sensitive Parliament
collapses

At such Heavy Questions.
Do not inquire
about the corpses
appearing here and there
of course, once in a way
Disappearances do Happen!
Hush! Don't worry!
just in case
The Power and Glory
of our King
that rises by the day
Shatters.

Hungry? Just a little patience!
don't you know?
this is only the effect
of a worldwide crisis.
Hush! Shut the Door!
stay Indoors …
Just in case
You expose
Our apprehensive government
shying away
in Stage Fright
from The People

Hear nothing!
See nothing!
Say nothing!
Until the little child
who saw through
the Emperor's Clothes
… Into the Nakedness,
Arrives
To
Awaken Us.

Mahesh Munasinge
Translated by Francesca Bremner

Excerpt from 'Seven Dreams'

Sixth Dream – As I was late, I missed you forever
I woke up in sorrowful vigilance.
Unaware, if it was early or late.
It was still dark.
All of a sudden, a feeling persisted
That someone somewhere was waiting for me.
Who and where was uncertain,
At times it might have been you.
The days ahead, the tasks and appointments,
Were torn off the calendar.
Only the months and days that had passed are remaining …

Walking along the A-9 road,[1]
I cleared the last military checkpoint,
Yet nowhere could I see you.
As I was late,
I did not know, if you had left.
I was in the Vanni,[2] but you were not there.
So I was sitting on the doorstep
Of a house in ruins
Waiting with your half of the cigarette …

Seventh Dream – The past shattered and floated away
Once the search operation had been completed,
The soldiers left.
And in the demolished room I found
Our group's last portrait
Torn into shreds.
Lingering on those time-faded scattered pieces
Was our smile
Of the last moments we spent together
Just before going our ways
Towards unknown destinies.
I placed the pieces on the window sill
Wanting to mend them.
A sudden mysterious wind
Stirred them up.

1. *The main north-south highway in Sri Lanka – leading into the war zone.*
2. *Vanni is the name for the rebel-held areas in the north where the war took place.*

Piece by piece they scattered
With the last autumn leaves
Moving to sites far away.
We had become tiny pieces of paper
Tumbling away in the wind.

Reflections on the Metamorphoses
Lying on a bed early at dawn,
Listening to the song of a bird
Is a dream
Which may collapse from a fatal scream
In yet another dream.

Who are you?
Dream by dream …
You follow me, while I follow you
And before we can meet
You escape
Only to reappear in different form.
Who are you?

Who are we?
Following each other, escaping each other again
Through the mountains, valleys and meadows
That once we crossed.
Who are we?
Thousands of metamorphoses in a single soul,
Thousands of souls in a single shape.

Even now,
I cannot distinguish myself from you,
As I cannot tell you apart from the others.
You are the prime universal matter,
While I am but the reflector.
With the second wave,
The corpses were flushed out to sea
And the swords were cleaned.
Everything but the difference

Between the quick and the dead
Was washed away ...

The nights they want to erase from our memory
Knock on the doors
Of wrecked houses full of bullet holes.
The dreams that were dreamt
During sleepless nights
Now are but short notes in an old diary ...
Paths never taken at the junction of indecision
Are blurring in the mist of time. ...

Ajith C Herath
Translated by Dawson Preethi and Karin Clark

(continues from page 170)

Elil views his poetry as a way of capturing the cultural memory of genocide. He is critical of those in his own community who betrayed the Tamil cause and now profit from the war. In his poem 'May 18th' [p. 171], the term Black July refers to the anti-Tamil pogrom in July 1983 which triggered full-scale civil war; Black May refers to the month when the war ended in the last rebel-held village of Mullivaikkal on the coast.

By contrast, Mahesh Munasinghe is a Sinhalese poet born in 1970. He started writing while actively involved in student politics in the late '80s and early 90s, heavily influenced by survivors of the leftist JVP (Sri Lankan People's Liberation Front) uprising in the south of the island. Mahesh emigrated to Canada in 2000 and went silent until he made a remarkable comeback in 2008, just as the civil war in Sri Lanka intensified. His poems were published online as well as in Sri Lankan newspapers and were read publicly at anti-war rallies and campaigns. Many readers circulated emails containing his poems as a way of expressing their opposition to the mass killing taking place in the north of Sri Lanka. Most of his work expresses the painful collective guilt experienced by those Sinhalese who opposed the war.

His poem 'Broken Pottu' [pp. 172–173] refers to the red spot, or pottu, traditionally worn by Hindu married women on their foreheads and more recently also by children to protect them from evil. Usually a widow stops wearing her pottu immediately after her husband's death, but in this war so many men have disappeared that women do not even know whether they are still entitled to wear it.

Ajith Herath, also Sinhalese, was born in 1967 and became involved in student politics during the JVP uprising in the 80s in the south of Sri Lanka. He was arrested by the military in 1989 and tortured, witnessing terrible brutality. Losing most of his close friends during that period of history, he learned to express his loss through poetry as a way of overcoming his own pain. While held in jail for almost three and half years, he wrote passionately and prolifically. His poems were frequently published in the alternative media in the first half of the 90s and he became one of the leading poets of his generation in the South. He is also a painter, political cartoonist and political analyst who worked as a journalist until he was forced into exile in 2008, when the civil war was reaching its denouement. Ajith received a scholarship and stayed at Böll House in Germany (affiliated to the Heinrich Böll Stifftüng) as a guest writer from May 2009 to January 2011.

His poem 'Seven Dreams' [pp. 176-178] blurs what happened in the past in the south with the recent killings of Tamils in the north, to show how it was the same army that conducted atrocities, first against an uprising by a youth movement and then by a minority. ❐

©Frances Harrison
41(2): 168/180
DOI: 10.1177/0306422012448171
www.indexoncensorship.org

Frances Harrison is a former BBC correspondent based in Sri Lanka 2000-4. Her book of survivors' stories from the end of the civil war, *Still Counting the Dead*, is published by Portobello Books later this year

12)WOMEX
THE WORLD MUSIC EXPO

GUIDE RATE
24 AUG
2012
DEADLINE

World & Jazz Networking
Trade Fair
Showcase Festival
Conference
Networking
Film Market
Awards
virtualWOMEX

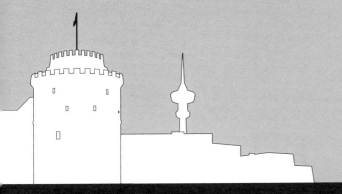

Thessaloniki, Greece
17–21 October 2012
www.womex.com

INDEX ON

£2.50 $4.30
Vol 22 No 1

CENSORSHIP

THE INTERNATIONAL MAGAZINE FOR FREE EXPRESSION

Vol 22 No 1

GENTLE
READER

After the relative liberalism of the 1970s, Judy Blume found her books for young adults on the censors' hit list

It never occurred to me, when I started to write more than 20 years ago, that what I was writing was controversial. Much of it grew out of my own feelings and concerns when I was young.

There were few challenges to my books then, although I remember the night a woman phoned, asking if I had written *Are You There God? It's Me, Margaret.* When I replied that I had, she called me a communist and slammed down the phone. I never did figure out if she equated communism with menstruation or religion, the two major concerns in 12-year-old Margaret's life.

But, in 1980, the censors crawled out of the woodwork, seemingly overnight, organised and determined. Not only would they decide what their children could read, but what all children could read. Challenges to books quadrupled within months, and we shall never know how many teachers, school librarians and principals quietly removed books to avoid trouble.

Censorship grows out of fear and, because fear is contagious, some parents are easily swayed. Book banning satisfies their need to feel in control of their children's lives. This fear is often disguised as moral outrage. They want to believe that if their children do not read about it, their children will not know about it. And if they do not know about it, it will not happen.

Today, it is not only language and sexuality (the usual reasons given for banning my books) that will land a book on the censors' hit list. It is Satanism, New Age-ism and a hundred other 'isms', some of which would be laughable if the implications were not so serious. Books that make kids laugh often come under suspicion; so do books that encourage kids to think, or question authority; books that don't hit the reader over the head with moral lessons are considered dangerous.

My book *Blubber* was banned in Montgomery County, Maryland, for 'lack of moral tone' and, more recently, challenged in Canton, Ohio, for allowing evil behaviour to go unpunished. But in New Zealand it is used in teacher-training classes to help explain classroom dynamics. Censors do not want children exposed to ideas different from their own. If every individual with an agenda had his or her way, the shelves in the school library would be close to empty.

But I am encouraged by a new awareness. This year I have received a number of letters from young people who are studying censorship in their classes. And in many communities across the country, students from elementary through to high school are becoming active (along with caring adults) in the fight to maintain their right to read and their right to choose books. They are speaking before school boards, and, more often than not, when they do, the books in question are returned to the shelves.

Only when readers of all ages become active, only when readers are willing to stand up to the censors, will the censors get the message that they cannot frighten us. ❑

©Judy Blume
41(2): 182/183
DOI: 10.1177/0306422012447739
www.indexoncensorship.org

Judy Blume writes books for readers of all ages